Nicole Pedersen-McKinnon

Double your wealth
and
Halve your worries
without the mumbo jumbo

Published by:
Wilkinson Publishing Pty Ltd
ACN 006 042 173
Level 4, 2 Collins Street
Melbourne, Vic 3000
Ph: 03 9654 5446

National Library of Australia Cataloguing-in-Publication data:

Pedersen-McKinnon, Nicole.

Double your wealth and halve your worries — without the mumbo jumbo.

ISBN 1 875889 892.

1. Saving and investment. 2. Investments. 3. Finance, Personal. I. Title.

332.02401

Cover and page design: qgraphics
Photography: Adam Hollingworth
Printed in Australia by McPherson's Printing Group, Maryborough, Australia

For Mrs Fiechtner. I finally did it – thank you.

And for the best proofing team in the world.
You know who you are and I love you all to bits.

About the Author

Nicole Pedersen-McKinnon launched and edits *The Australian Financial Review's Investor* liftout, which appears in *The Sun-Herald* and *The Sunday Age*, as well as the news-stand magazine, *AFR Smart Investor*.

She is an award-winning journalist, named Pensions and Investment Journalist of the Year while working in the United Kingdom for the magazine arm of the *Financial Times* and, since returning to Australia, taking out the personal finance category of the Citigroup Journalism Awards for Excellence.

Finally, Nicole is both a qualified financial adviser and qualified stock broker. She has provided expert commentary on radio and television in Australia and in the United Kingdom, and addressed investment audiences in the United States.

A Word from Nicole

If there's one thing I've learnt from my time as a personal finance journalist and editor, it's just how distressing money can be. Almost daily, I get emails and phone calls from readers urgently seeking my help in managing it, saving it, growing it and protecting it.

The whole process is made all the more traumatic by the sheer complexity of the available information and advice. Call me a conspiracy theorist, but I think that's how the financial community likes it – let's face it, the less you know about managing your money, the more likely you are to have to pay one of its members to do it for you.

Well, enough. It's high time that *everyone* knew the very simple secrets to building wealth, along with the traps that – although easily avoidable – have the potential to destroy all your good work.

Into this short book I have condensed everything I've ever been taught, every bit of research I've ever done and every piece of advice I've ever written. I've also included my Top Tips – and companies' Dirty Tricks.

Don't waste time worrying about your finances – take control of them instead!

Nicole Pedersen-McKinnon

Table of Contents

Step 1
Get your relationship with money right

Let's get one thing straight right at the outset – you control your money, it doesn't control you. Remember that and you have the battle half won.

For so many people, money is an incredibly emotional issue. Each week I am contacted by at least a dozen readers desperate for help getting out of a tight financial spot.

But if you think it's only stressful if you don't have enough money, think again – it's a well-known fact that people with little experience of money who suddenly come into a sizeable sum can become consumed with fear about losing it!

So with that in mind, focus on getting your attitude to money right and learn to look at your financial situation from an unemotional perspective. I guarantee that if you allow your psychological wellbeing to be tied up in the ebb and flow of your bank account, not only will it get you down more than it should if you're going through a lean patch, but you risk blowing it all as therapy when things turn around.

Really, the secret to realising your wealth potential is similar to the secret to keeping your weight down: avoid the denial/binge cycle. In other words, be too strict on yourself and you're bound to head for the nearest Westfield and/or biscuit tin. You'll no doubt be pleased to hear I advocate moderation not deprivation.

When it's a team effort

Of course, it helps a great deal if both people in a relationship are equally focused on increasing their wealth. There's nothing more frustrating than finding a joint bank account is empty once again when you have been exercising extreme spending restraint.

On this front, I am very lucky. Perhaps it's years of me droning on about the importance of stockpiling for the future, but my husband, Daniel, is just as committed to achieving our financial goals as I am (he'll also be very pleased I have finally mentioned him in print. He's been suggesting I write about him for years!). I am definitely more stingy – I consider it an occupational hazard – but he is very willing to make short-term sacrifices in the name of building our long-term wealth.

Something else to bear in mind is that, as personally rewarding as kids may be, financially rewarding they are not. Just like pets, they eat up significant, unpredictable amounts of cash. So if you can get any debt under control before you have them, as Daniel and I are trying to do, you will be much more likely to realise your wealth potential.

Don't despair if it's too late for that, though. Your journey may simply take a little longer.

The high cost of complacency

You might think the biggest threat to your wealth is some unforseen disaster, but it's actually inertia. That's right – failing to implement a

> If you've had the same credit card
> for a few years now, chances are
> you are being ripped off

financial strategy, failing to stick to that strategy, failing to amend it for changing economic and market conditions *and* failing to take advantage of great new deals.

Fierce competition in both utilities and financial services means that offers are getting better almost daily.

And I know from personal experience just how much you can save...

Utilities

When Daniel and I moved just recently (when we purchased our very first home), we found we could get a *faster* internet connection with *more* download capacity for *less* than we were paying before. $20 less, to be exact. However, the really amazing thing was that this was from the very same provider we were already using.

But we decided not to. The reason? Because further research revealed we could actually connect wireless broadband for the same $50 a month we were used to paying. And that meant we could do without a land line.

You see, we were already using our pre-pay mobiles for the majority of our calls anyway because, with most of our Australian family and friends on the same network, they were either free or the cost was negligible. However, we were still paying about $50 a month for the landline – partly for the odd non-mobile call but mostly just so we could have access to the internet.

So we connected Voice over Internet Protocol (VoIP), technology that allows you to make cheap as chips voice calls over the internet (it's especially good for international calls), signed up for wireless broadband – and cut the cord to Telstra.

We also realised we weren't getting value from our capped mobile plans – plans that give you, for example, $250 worth of credit for $49. Most months they were expiring with unused credit. So we switched to cheaper deals.

In all, our so-called 'fixed' costs fell by almost $100 a month, simply because we bothered to check the available offers.

Don't waste time worrying about your finances
– take control of them instead!

Wealth watch

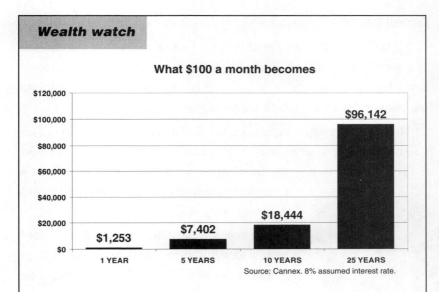

What $100 a month becomes

Source: Cannex. 8% assumed interest rate.

If, like us, you can manage to shave $100 a month off your bills, and you invest that money at 8 per cent, you'll have $1253 after one year, $7402 after five, $18,444 after 10 and an incredible $96,142 after 25 (all savings examples assume interest is paid monthly).

These figures show the powerful effect of compound interest, a mathematical phenomenon that Albert Einstein once referred to as the 8th wonder of the world.

But it's also worth thinking about the numbers from the opposite perspective. If you want to retire at age 60, you will have $1253 if you start saving $100 a month at age 59, $7402 if you start at age 55, $18,444 if you start at age 50 and a much more impressive $96,142 if you start at age 35.

Obviously, the higher the amount you can spare and the earlier you can start putting this away, the more money you will amass. So get cracking!

Credit cards

If you've had the same credit card for a few years now, chances are you are being ripped off. These days the competition among banks is fierce because more and more overseas players are trying to break into our market. As a result, there are some great deals on offer.

Not only are standard interest rates coming down, but in many cases you can transfer your existing balance and pay absolutely no interest

on it for up to six months. This gives you a fantastic opportunity to clear your credit card debt once and for all.

We recently switched to a different card purely to get a better deal on frequent flyer points (1 point for each $1 spent rather than 1 point for each $1.50). It's true collecting points isn't such good value anymore, but we had virtually no furniture when we bought our apartment, and planned to buy each item on the card the month before we actually had the money. I figured we may as well get a bonus for all that spending!

However, I was stunned when I called to cancel our existing card that they agreed in an instant – without even making a half-hearted attempt to keep our business. From everything I had heard from family, friends and readers, I had expected them to offer me all sorts of concessions to try to retain us as customers. Why didn't they? I strongly suspect because we clear our balance every month so they had *never* made any money out of us. On the computer screen probably popped up the message 'good riddance'!

Do you need any further evidence that finance companies are out not for you but for themselves?

But I digress. Let's get back to the improved deals on offer

Online savings accounts

For any money you need to keep safe, it's hard to go past an online savings account. Nowadays, these accounts offer the highest interest of any deposit accounts, even those where you lock your money away in order to secure a better rate. Be aware, however, that with some you may not be able to access your cash instantly, but have to wait a couple of days.

Don't be frightened by the online part either. These accounts are so easy to open I would be surprised if it took you more than 20 minutes (if I, as a complete technophobe, can do it, you definitely can). And banks are spending huge amounts of money to ensure your online transactions are safe (we'll get into the simple precautions you can follow to protect yourself from online fraud in Step 8).

For the best rates on credit cards and online savings accounts today, go to www.cannex.com.au or www.infochoice.com.au. It's worth having a look pretty regularly too – bigger and better deals are coming out all the time.

Top Tips

> Don't tie yourself into *any* telecommunications contract. Competition is so hot among providers right now that a better deal is bound to be just around the corner.

> Consider whether you really need that landline. Mobile phone deals have become incredibly competitive (particularly for STD calls and calls to other mobiles), and wireless broadband means you no longer have to be a hostage to Telstra.

> If you have broadband, it costs next to nothing (the price of a headset) to hook up VoIP through your personal computer, and you can then make dirt cheap STD and international phone calls to a landline, or free calls to someone else with VoIP. (Incidentally, you may be interested to learn that this technology has been around for many years but is only now taking off in Australia because previously the speed of the average home internet connection was too slow.)

> Once you have established your various methods of communicating with the outside world, make sure you use each deal to its best advantage. For instance, if you need to make an overseas call, use VoIP rather than your landline or mobile. Make your arrangement work for you.

> Look at how you can cut your utilities bills. For example:

  o Paying a little extra for energy-efficient appliances is well worth it in the long run (for both your wallet and the environment).

  o Remember also that clothes dryers are notorious energy suckers – we live in a bright sunny country anyway!

  o And, according to EnergyAustralia, the average household pays 5-10 per cent more for electricity than it should simply because appliances are left on stand-by. Turn them off at the wall.

> If you find a better credit card, be sure to cut up your old one. There's no sense in increasing the temptation to spend.

> Also, beware of switching cards *too* many times – under Australia's credit reporting system, the number of credit applications you make is recorded and could well give the impression you have a problem dealing with debt, and go against you when making future applications for credit. Once or twice a year should be fine.

> Still on credit cards, here's a cheeky idea:

1. Get the biggest cash advance possible from your existing credit card then immediately transfer your balance to a card that will charge 0 per cent on that debt for a period of time.

2. Put the cash into the online bank account paying the highest interest rate.

3. Just before the interest-free period on your new credit card expires, withdraw the money from your online account and pay off the card.

You won't make a fortune because you will be limited as to how much cash you can withdraw on the credit card – but you can't scoff at money for nothing.

Dirty tricks

> Companies routinely rely on the customers who are on old plans to fund the great discounts they offer on new ones. They just hope you won't realise it.

Defence: Get on the phone and find out if prices have come down since you signed up. Threaten to take your business elsewhere if they refuse to let you switch plans.

> Very rarely do you actually get 55 days interest-free – or whatever is the advertised interest-free period (some cards now offer 62). This is only the *maximum* number of interest-free days. It's usually made up of the month between statements plus 25 days to pay the bill. So, depending on the timing of your purchases, you can get as few as 25 days interest-free.

Defence: Know exactly from which date the interest-free days apply – to make matters more complex, it can be statement date, the first day of the month or even each individual purchase date. If it's going to take you the full 55 (or 62) days to pay off the item, make sure you buy it on day one of your interest-free period (for example, if your statement is posted on the 15th of every month, make the purchase on the 16th).

> Be aware that, with 0 per cent balance transfer cards, there is no interest-free period on any new spending. Such purchases will accrue interest from day one, and keep accruing interest until you have paid off your transferred balance.

Defence: Don't use your card until you have repaid your balance. If you absolutely must use credit in this period, use a card that will give you interest-free days.

> Still on balance transfer cards, once the introductory period ends, the rate on what you've rolled over may well become uncompetitive.

Defence: Check. If at that stage you can get a better deal elsewhere, switch again (making sure not to switch *too* many times).

> Some online savings accounts offer a knockout interest rate – but only for a limited period of time.

Defence: By all means take advantage of the high rate, but jump ship once another account offers you a better deal (you can do this as many times as you like without repercussion).

Useful Websites

Telecommunications comparisons:

www.phonechoice.com.au (an independent analyst with a bill calculator) and www.cheapphonedeals.com.au (a free phone broker).

Financial products comparisons:

www.cannex.com.au and www.infochoice.com.au

Step 2
Know your debt intimately

You might have heard the terms good debt and bad debt. Well I prefer to call them **Alright Debt** and **Very Bloody Bad Debt**. And, with our brand new home loan, we have far too much Very Bloody Bad Debt for my liking. So we're throwing absolutely everything we can at it – and so should you (at your own I mean, although donations gratefully accepted).

Any Very Bloody Bad Debt is holding you back from realising your wealth potential. But by channelling all your spare cash in its direction, you are effectively earning a return equivalent to the interest rate you are being charged. And, unlike if you invested the money instead, you don't pay any tax on these 'earnings'.

What all that means is that, to *equal* the benefit of putting your spare cash on a mortgage with an 8 per cent interest rate, a higher rate taxpayer would need to earn 15.5 per cent (and if you know how to do that risk-free then you are doing better than I am!).

So first paying off any Very Bloody Bad Debt – let's call it VBBD for short – is a no-brainer.

> Credit cards and personal loans are the
> worst categories of VBBD

Very bad VBBD

Credit cards and personal loans are the worst categories of VBBD because not only are the interest rates usually higher than a mortgage, but they are mainly used for depreciating assets – assets that are going to fall in value – or experiences you've forgotten long before you have repaid what you owe. This type of debt needs to be your number one priority because, unlike a mortgage, the assets you are paying off are doing nothing to increase your wealth.

Credit cards

Never make only the required monthly payment on a credit card as – even if you don't spend another cent – your debt could *grow*.

Let's assume you routinely carry over a debt of $2000, at an interest rate of 17.65 per cent, on a card with a minimum monthly repayment of 1.5 per cent (so $30) and a $59 annual fee that you roll into your balance. (By the way, this is an actual card – I haven't just plucked these figures out of the air).

Twenty-five years later you will owe not $2000 but *$3242*, says Cannex. And you will have paid $11,970 in interest to that point.

This is due to the combination of a high interest rate, moderate annual fee and low minimum monthly repayment. You won't hear the bank complaining though. They will make more and more over time.

Cannex calculates that you will still have debt in 25 years (again assuming a $2000 balance) if your card has an interest rate of 16 per cent or more (a bit higher than average), an annual fee of $24 (relatively low) and a minimum repayment of 2 per cent or less (about normal).

Unless of course you pay more than the minimum – or even better, get a card with a lower rate and no (or a low) annual fee, and pay more than the minimum anyway. After all, you don't want to still be paying off a jacket bought today in 2030.

If you can't afford to pay your balance in full each month, you shouldn't be using credit.

As mentioned in Step 1, the very best way to clear an existing credit card debt is to open one of the cards offering an interest rate of 0 per cent for a period of time on transferred balances. This is like a 'get out of jail free' card because it gives you the opportunity to repay your debt much more quickly. So transfer that balance and then move heaven and earth to clear it within the interest-free period.

Personal loans

The interest rate on personal loans is typically higher than on ordinary mortgages because they are secured not over property but over a depreciating asset, such as a car – or sometimes not secured at all.

However, there is actually a positive aspect to these loans – unlike with credit cards, you borrow money for a pre-determined period. You may have, for example, four years to repay the debt and your repayments will be set accordingly.

But you will still pay a fair whack of interest over the time, which is why you should never sign up for a loan on which you cannot accelerate repayments to pay off your debt more quickly (make sure, too, that there are no penalties for clearing the loan early).

Beyond this, another strategy to pay down your debt fast is to roll any credit card debts that you are unable to repay within the available 0 per cent balance transfer periods into a lower-interest personal loan. The beauty of this is that, unlike with a credit card, you will have a specified time in which to pay your debt off.

A further option is to roll both your credit card debts *and* your personal loans into your mortgage. However, here you must keep your repayments at the level you were paying before. If you drop them to the minimum required under your home loan, you will ultimately pay more in interest because it will take you longer to repay your debt.

Just bear in mind that if you choose to roll your debts into your mortgage but you then have trouble meeting the repayments, your lender could come after your house.

Interest-free finance

It's well worth mentioning interest-free finance here. No deposit and no interest for a period of time probably sound like a great deal, but if you miss a payment by so much as one day, you could be charged an eye-watering interest rate (as high as 30 per cent) – back to day one! It could even be the same deal if you owe anything at all when the interest-free period expires.

Don't assume that you'll pay off the item before then if you simply make the minimum monthly repayments, though – these will be set low enough to ensure that the lender will make money from you.

In fact, companies that offer this type of credit are often *trying* to trip you up. Why do I say that? Because I know of not one but two cases where people have been refused credit because their credit records were too good! In other words, they were likely to adhere strictly to the contract and pay off the loan before interest became due. So the lenders weren't interested.

Also remember, just because it's interest-free doesn't mean it's *fee-free*. I have heard of an instance where there was a $30 establishment fee, then an $8 a month admin fee. This actually equated to an interest rate of nearly 10 per cent.

Do your sums. Better still, save the money first and go shopping second.

Necessary VBBD

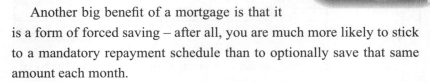

While a mortgage does fall into the VBBD category, think of it as a tool to build your wealth. As you pay it off, the property will hopefully be increasing in value. And the faster you clear your debt, the less money you pay in interest.

Another big benefit of a mortgage is that it is a form of forced saving – after all, you are much more likely to stick to a mandatory repayment schedule than to optionally save that same amount each month.

But if you are considering taking out a mortgage, you need to be extremely careful you don't borrow too much. Most finance companies will lend you about five times your salary (for a couple, this will be less but based on your combined salaries). So, if you earn $40,000, you might be able to borrow $200,000.

However, just because this is how much you *can* get, doesn't mean it is how much you *should* get. Remember, institutions are out for themselves, not for you – and you need to make sure you are not creating problems for yourself down the track.

A good rule of thumb is to keep your borrowing to a level that you can repay each month with 30 per cent of your before-tax salary (not including super), as either a single or a couple.

Another vital test is to know how you would cope if your repayments went up. The table below will show you how they will increase or decrease with interest rates. Simply find the amount you intend to borrow (or have borrowed) down the side, and the current interest rate along the top – and look to the square where the columns meet. As you can see, a 0.5 of a percentage point increase in the interest rate on a $250,000 loan means about an extra $80 a month.

Monthly repayments on a 25-year loan

Loan amount	Interest rate %							
	6.00	6.50	7.00	7.50	8.00	8.50	9.00	9.50
$50,000	$322	$338	$353	$369	$386	$403	$420	$437
$100,000	$644	$675	$707	$739	$772	$805	$839	$874
$150,000	$966	$1,013	$1,060	$1,108	$1,158	$1,208	$1,259	$1,311
$200,000	$1,289	$1,350	$1,414	$1,478	$1,544	$1,610	$1,678	$1,747
$250,000	$1,611	$1,688	$1,767	$1,847	$1,930	$2,013	$2,098	$2,184
$300,000	$1,933	$2,026	$2,120	$2,217	$2,315	$2,416	$2,518	$2,621
$350,000	$2,255	$2,363	$2,474	$2,586	$2,701	$2,818	$2,937	$3,058
$400,000	$2,577	$2,701	$2,827	$2,956	$3,087	$3,221	$3,357	$3,495
$450,000	$2,899	$3,038	$3,181	$3,325	$3,473	$3,624	$3,776	$3,932
$500,000	$3,222	$3,376	$3,534	$3,695	$3,859	$4,026	$4,196	$4,368

Source: Infochoice.com.au

Think about how you would fare meeting that additional cost today. What if your circumstances changed? Say you went from a two-income to a one-income household for a while, perhaps because you start a family? Look at affordability in every contingency.

Also consider taking the loan not over 25 years but over 30 years. We have. This keeps our required repayments as low as possible and affords some protection should our circumstances take a turn for the worst. Of course, the idea is to still pay as much as you can each month – if you don't you will simply end up paying more interest (because it's the same rate over a longer period) and so be well behind in your quest to double your wealth.

Wealth watch

Here's food for thought if you are considering abandoning renting to purchase a home of your own: if you do and the property market simply moves sideways, or slumps and then recovers to where it is now, the move could see you more than $70,000 out of pocket in five years' time.

According to figures calculated by Infochoice, house prices would need to increase by at least 3 per cent a year in each of the next five years to make buying worthwhile. And, if you had to pay stamp duty on your purchase, prices would need to go up that much more for you to come out ahead.

But if prices increased 5 per cent a year your equity would increase enormously – in fact, you would probably be $50,000 better off.

We've assumed that you buy a house valued at $450,000 (with a 10 per cent deposit) or pay rent on that house of $400 a week. Over five years, that puts your house repayments at $172,834 (at 7.07 per cent interest) or your rent at $109,437 (if it escalates by 2.5 per cent a year). Note that the rent does not even cover *interest* payments on the mortgage.

But, of course, there are extra costs associated with being a home owner. We've allowed for total rates and (possibly) body corporate payments of $7000 over five years and an annual maintenance bill of $2000, which takes your total expense as a home owner to $189,834.

Finally, we've assumed – and this is the *big* assumption – that you diligently save all of the extra money you would have paid on a mortgage and maintaining your house (and earned 5 per cent a year on it). If you managed to do that, you would be looking at $150,943 additional cash in the bank (including the $45,000 deposit). This compares with equity in a house at that stage of $80,463 – $35,463 that you would have paid off and the $45,000 deposit.

However, if you didn't diligently put aside the money you saved by renting, buying would mean you really miss out. Besides, should house prices take off again, renters will be left behind.

Pay it down fast

If you're deep into a mortgage, you'll be much more interested in how to discharge your debt as quickly as possible. I hate to be the bearer of bad news but the only real way is to make extra mortgage repayments.

However, there are some strategies that will help ...

• Trick yourself into it

One of the very best approaches is to trick yourself into making extra repayments – and it's easier than you think thanks to our calendar. Now stay with me here.

There are 12 months in a year. Yes? However, there are not (12 x 2) 24 fortnights, but 26. And there are not (12 x 4) 48 weeks, but 52.

What does all that mean? Well, if you are paid fortnightly, and from each pay make *half* your minimum monthly repayments, you will be ahead by one month every year (because there are not 24 but 26 fortnights in a year).

Similarly, if you are paid weekly, and you make *one quarter* of your minimum monthly repayments, you will also be ahead by one month every year (because there are not 48 but 52 weeks in a year).

You are unlikely to miss the small amount of money you are putting in extra each time, but it will make a big difference to your bottom line. Let's say you have a $250,000 mortgage with minimum monthly repayments of $1472. If you paid half that amount each fortnight – $736 – instead of the $679 that would be required, you would save four years and five months of a 25-year term and an estimated $59,000, according to Cannex.

• Offset or redraw

Another strategy that is well worth it, is to park any savings you might have lying around (half your luck) either in your mortgage or into an offset account, a savings account that runs parallel to your mortgage and gives you a dollar-for-dollar reduction in the interest on your mortgage.

If you were to leave $10,000 sitting from day one on our example $250,000 mortgage, Cannex says it would save you two years and six months and more than $43,000. You would also earn a higher effective return on your $10,000, remembering this is tax-free, than you would by putting the money into a no-risk savings account.

• Get a better deal

Keep an eagle eye on home loan interest rates – by monitoring advertisements and the Cannex and Infochoice websites – and consider switching mortgages if there is a better deal on offer. Then keep contributing the same amount and you will pay off your loan a whole lot faster.

If you moved from paying 8 per cent on a $250,000 loan to paying 7.5 per cent, but kept your repayments the same, you would save 2.8 years and $65,102.

It's also worth keeping a close watch on fixed rates throughout your loan term. If they move more than two interest rate cuts below your variable rate (so 0.5 of a percentage point), consider fixing half your loan and, again, maintaining your repayments at the same level – such an interest rate saving for even a few years can cut $10,000 or more off your mortgage.

Just watch that if you remortgage you won't incur exit penalties so high that it will cancel out the benefit (see Dirty Tricks at the end of this Step).

● The credit card myth

Getting paid into any sort of transactional mortgage (all-in-one mortgage, line of credit etc) and using a credit card for your expenses really isn't worth it. The idea is to shift the money from your mortgage onto your credit card only when your bill becomes due, so saving interest on the mortgage.

Despite all the hype around this strategy, the saving is tiny at only a few thousand dollars on a $250,000 loan at 8 per cent, assuming you are paid $1500 after tax a fortnight. The only time this might make a big difference is if your home loan is especially small and/or your salary is especially big.

It makes sense if you think about it – you only ever have the equivalent of one extra pay sitting on your mortgage. How much impact can this really have?

Regardless, there are plenty of 'debt reduction' services out there willing to put a credit card strategy in place for you for a modest sum of up to $6000 – yes, for a saving of possibly only a few thousand dollars. They have lots of fancy charts to 'prove' it works, but all these show is the effect of making extra repayments. Don't be sucked in.

One final word on this strategy, and indeed any type of transactional mortgage: you need to be extremely disciplined to ensure you don't simply go backwards. By having your mortgage as your working account, you will be able to dip into your equity at any time. To me, that's just dangerous. Give me a plain vanilla, principal and interest mortgage any day.

Wealth watch

The effect of extra repayments on a $250,000 mortgage

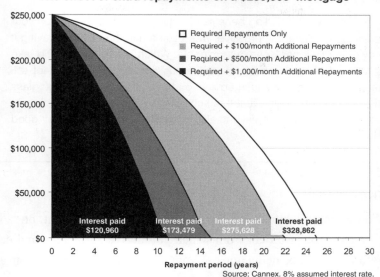

Source: Cannex. 8% assumed interest rate.

Every extra dollar you put on your mortgage comes straight off the principal and therefore increases your wealth. The chart above shows the effect of paying $100, $500 and $1000 above the minimum monthly repayment on a $250,000 loan at 8 per cent (taken over 25 years). As you can see ...

> $100 saves you three years and four months, and more than $53,000;

> $500 saves you 10 years and five months, and more than $155,000, and;

> $1000 saves you 14 years and five months, and a remarkable $207,902.

It's also worth looking at this another way ... Taking the example where you pay an extra $100 a month, by forking out only $26,000 over the life of the loan you save $53,234. So, for every $1 you have put on your mortgage, you have saved just over $2 in interest. The saving per dollar slightly decreases with the higher repayments – but so does the time it takes to repay the mortgage. (Source: Infochoice.)

While the wealth-building benefits of putting extra repayments on your mortgage really are impressive, when you are in the midst of paying it down, the task can seem interminable. Which is why you should take a leaf out of my Mum's book and focus not on how much debt still remains, but on how much equity you have already built. It's a 'glass half full' way of looking at it that should allow you some satisfaction at your ongoing achievement and also motivate you to keep up your good work.

Alright debt

You'll hear a bunch of finance professionals say that on any investment debt – so debt from which you derive an income and can therefore claim tax deductions – your repayments should be on an interest-only basis.

The strategy is most often touted in connection with negatively geared investments – in other words, investments where your interest and other costs (such as repairs on an investment property) exceed the income from that investment (such as rent).

The idea is to keep your interest high by ensuring your loan balance stays the same and therefore maximise your tax deductions for interest.

Well, there are a few flaws in this approach. The biggest is that you are out of pocket each and every month. Yes, the government chips in (in the form of a tax refund) but only to the extent of your marginal tax rate – so 16.5 per cent, 31.5 per cent or 48.5 per cent (NB. The strategy is more effective in higher tax brackets). *You* need to find the rest.

It wasn't until I calculated some figures in conjunction with the National Tax and Accountants Association that I realised just how expensive this strategy can be.

Let's assume you are a higher-rate taxpayer – so get the maximum benefit from negative gearing – and have a $250,000 loan for an investment property at 7.07 per cent interest over 25 years.

After 25 years with a principal and interest (P&I) loan you'll have paid $395,970, taking into account the tax saving, and *own* the $250,000 property. But with an interest-only loan you'll have paid $227,566, also taking into account the tax saving, and *still owe* $250,000.

The difference between the $395,970 net layout with P&I and the $227,566 net layout with interest-only represents the $305.20 a month you've saved in repayments by going interest-only ($91,561 overall) and the extra tax deductions you've earned by maintaining your debt at the same level ($76,843).

However, this $168,404 total saving falls short of the $250,000 you need to buy the property and get into the same position as you would have been with a P&I loan – by $81,596.

So despite obtaining a greater tax deduction under an interest-only loan, you will pay less money overall under a principal and interest loan.

Of course, the idea is that when you sell a negatively geared investment you will have a big fat capital gain that will make up for all the money you have forked out. But what if the market is flat and you make nothing? Or, even worse, you lose money? Excuse the very poor pun but, in an uncertain market, you could be dicing with debt.

The more equity you build up via P&I repayments, the more you are protecting yourself. Besides, you are trying to increase your wealth – so it's much better for you and *not* the bank to own the asset.

The exception to the rule

The only time I *am* a believer in interest-only is if you still have VBBD (or bad debt if you want to be conventional about it), such as a home loan. The interest on this debt is not tax deductible – therefore it's doing nothing but eating into your income.

However, by paying interest-only on any investment debt you will free up a bit of cash, which you can then use to knock off your VBBD faster. And a side benefit is that this will keep your deductions high.

After you've cleared your home loan, you can switch back to paying P&I on your investments, and continue your previous wealth-building mission.

Let's take the previous example a bit further, and assume you have an outstanding home loan, which carries no tax advantage whatsoever, as well as a $250,000 investment property.

If you take out an interest-only investment loan and put the $305.20 you save each month towards a $250,000 home loan (P&I), you'd save $98,814 in interest and cut seven years and seven months off your mortgage.

Netting off this $98,814 saving against the $81,596 extra cost of the interest-only investment loan (remember, the amount that you still needed to find to pay off the property?) you're $17,218 ahead.

But the *actual* result will be even better because, from year 17, you'll have an additional $2083 a month (the $1778 minimum home loan repayment plus the $305.20 you've been overpaying) to use to start building equity in your investment property.

Top tips

> Remember, if you are able to save a deposit of 20 per cent of the purchase price of a house *and* you also have cash for costs – usually a further 5 per cent – you won't be forced to pay lenders' mortgage insurance. Contrary to what many people believe, this does not cover your mortgage repayments if you get into trouble. Instead, it covers your lender if they cannot recoup what you owe them from the forced sale of your house. And it's an upfront payment of up to 3.5 per cent of the loan value; if you borrow 95 per cent of a $250,000 property, it would usually be about 1.75 per cent, which works out at $4156. Much better to put the money towards your equity instead.

> When you buy one property and sell another, you actually end up losing more like 10 per cent in costs (including real estate agent's fees and moving expenses). So make sure you can stay in one property at least until it grows in value by this amount.

> Don't sign up for any mortgage that doesn't let you pay extra (and make sure interest is calculated daily so you get the full effect of these repayments).

> Also, check if you qualify for what is called a professional package. This is a type of loan originally available to doctors, lawyers and the like, but now open to anyone with a salary of more than about $50,000 who is borrowing more than about $150,000. It will generally give you an interest rate discount of between 0.4 and 0.7 of a percentage point. However, because the loan usually comes with a 'package' of products, for example, a credit card and transaction account, there is an annual fee of up to $300. So be sure the discount is worth it.

> Fix your rate only if you can get an interest rate lower than the variable rate, only on half your mortgage and only for a maximum of three years – a lot can happen even in that time.

> If interest rates go down, keep paying the same. Unless you are having real trouble making ends meet, you should only ever *increase* your mortgage repayments. (Once you pay off the loan,

save the same amount so your wealth keeps growing.)

> With any offset account, check that you earn the same rate as on your mortgage, on 100 per cent of your savings.

> If there is any chance you will want to turn a home on which you have a mortgage into an investment property down the track, make any extra repayments into an offset account. Otherwise, you will lose deductions for what you have already repaid.

> It is safest to invest in property that is positively geared (where the rent covers your expenses), has positive cash flow (where the rent plus your tax refund covers your expenses) or is likely to become positively geared in the shorter term (because of decreasing costs, increasing rent or both). However, the caveat here is that you need to be confident it will also at least maintain its value.

> Because any negatively geared investment means money out of your pocket, ensure you don't overextend yourself and only enter into such an arrangement if you think the prospect of a capital gain is good (so you stand a chance of getting your outlay back).

> Don't dip into the equity in your house for depreciating assets or lifestyle expenditure, such as holidays. It is not a slush fund – it is the main source of your future financial security.

Dirty tricks

> Any loan with an introductory or honeymoon rate is likely to become uncompetitive at the end of the period in which this applies.

Defence: Make sure to find out what's called the revert rate. If this is higher than other products, forget about it – an initial discount will never make up for a higher rate over the rest of the loan.

> Some lenders keep interest rates artificially low by levying fees instead. A small monthly fee on a mortgage product or a moderate annual fee on a credit card will quickly cancel out the effect of a lower interest rate.

Defence: Avoid such products.

> Along these lines, mortgage providers have actually *invented* a new fee to make their interest rates look more competitive. Called a deferred establishment fee it loads costs into the back end if you leave. This form of 'early' repayment fee is now levied by 40 per cent of lenders and can apply for up to the first five years, even though Fujitsu Consulting says the average mortgage is in place only 3.7 years. And it can be up to 2 per cent of the original loan value — so if the loan was for $250,000, it would be $5000. Non-bank lenders are the worst culprits, and you could still have to pay exit, settlement and legal fees.

Defence: Don't remortgage or pay out a loan before you've checked whether you'll be slugged. It could be that it works out best to wait, or to move to a new mortgage from the same financial institution, in which case the fee will not apply. Better still, don't take out such a product in the first place.

> If, in a bid to trick yourself into making an extra monthly repayment each year (as outlined on page 18), you approach your bank and ask to switch your repayments from monthly to fortnightly or weekly, be aware that they will adjust them down to ensure it still takes you the full 25 or 30 years to repay your loan.

Defence: Determine how much you need to pay yourself. It's really easy — if you want to pay fortnightly, simply halve your minimum monthly repayment and, if you want to pay weekly, divide it by four.

> Although the process of choosing a mortgage can be made much easier by using a mortgage broker, be aware that they may offer a choice of only a limited number of lenders. They are also paid a commission by the chosen institution so can be influenced by the amount of this commission.

Defence: Ensure any broker you are considering has at least 20 lenders on its panel, ask to see the commissions paid by each and never, ever hand over any money yourself. In fact, if you are feeling bold, ask them to rebate some of their commission to you! You might be able to cover your moving costs. Also, make sure any broker you are considering is registered with the Mortgage Industry Association of Australia. Go to www.miaa. com.au and do a 'MIAA accredited members search'.

> See the bit on debt reduction services on page 20 – never pay anyone for a debt reduction strategy.

Defence: Put the money on the mortgage instead.

> Even if you honour your loan contract and stay with the same institution until the bitter end, you will have to pay a fee. Mortgage discharge fees can run to a few hundred dollars.

Defence: I am afraid there is none – just be aware it's coming!

Useful websites

Mortgage Industry Association of Australia website:
www.miaa.com.au

Information on buying and selling property:
www.reiaustralia.com.au (Real Estate Institute of Australia) and www.realestate.com.au

Financial products comparisons:
www.cannex.com.au and www.infochoice.com.au

Consumer protection website:
www.consumer.gov.au (Ministerial Council on Consumer Affairs). See also the website for your state's Office of Fair Trading.

Financial counselling:
www.fido.asic.gov.au (this website is run by the Australian Securities and Investments Commission. Search for 'financial counselling' to bring up a contact number for a service in your state).

Step 3
Make every cent you can

There is no better way to give your finances a boost than to increase your income – a pay rise will immediately improve your personal bottom line and dramatically hasten the speed with which you can double your wealth (assuming, of course, you don't simply absorb it with new spending – but we'll get to that in Step 4).

And it's not as difficult to secure as you think.

Bailing up the boss

Ask and you shall receive. Or so the saying goes. In reality, you might not receive – but you stand a far better chance than if you wait for your boss to be feeling benevolent.

While every employee is entitled to have their salary reviewed at least annually, the process is one that's easily deferred – either temporarily or sometimes even permanently. If reviews don't happen automatically in your workplace, take control and initiate that discussion yourself.

At the very least, each year you should get an inflationary pay rise of between 2 and 3 per cent to ensure the real value of your income is not eroded over time.

But if you feel you are excelling in your job, it won't hurt to bring that to your manager's attention – and ask for a merit-based pay increase in recognition.

Here, the manner of your approach will be vital. First collect evidence of the strong contribution you are making to the company – such as sales figures, revenue against your targets, customer feedback and any other measurable performance indicator. Then present this to your boss along with a calm and reasoned case as to why you think you deserve a pay rise.

If you are a valued employee and they believe you are doing a good job, they are very likely to accede to your request. Your employer won't want to lose you – or, looking at it more cynically, incur the cost of recruiting someone to replace you.

But if they do say no, don't *immediately* start scouring the employment pages. Bide your time for a while. I would bet that, because you've brought your situation to their attention, you'll be much more likely to get an increase in the next round of pay reviews.

Changing jobs

The very best way of getting a pay rise is to either win a promotion or move to a different organisation.

Once the decision has been made that you are the right person for the job, you are in a strong position of control – they want *you* so tell them in no uncertain terms what it is that you want. Provided it's realistic, this is your opportunity to secure a significant increase in your salary.

> The very best way of getting a pay rise is to either win a promotion or move to a different organisation

In a way, the longer you are in a job, the more 'invisible' you become – in other words, the less likely you are to receive financial recognition of your contribution. However, once this is brought to your employer's attention by a rival job offer, who knows, they might even be willing to up your pay in order to keep you. Nothing fattens the pay packet like an old-fashioned bidding war.

Taking on extra work

Another option is to take on extra work, such as overtime, or get a part-time job on the side. While this is going to cut into your spare time, if the money is right, you might decide it's worth it. Just be aware that you will be taxed more heavily on a second job.

Looking long term

The final way to increase your earning capacity is to skill up – so take every opportunity to boost your qualifications. Sign up for any workplace training offered through your employer and even consider undertaking some study off your own bat.

While you are likely to have to pay for any external study, it may be tax deductible if related to your current source of income. However, if your chosen course is in an unrelated field, with a view to a complete career change, view it as an investment in yourself. Over time, it should pay for itself over and over.

Wealth watch

What $500 and $600 a month becomes

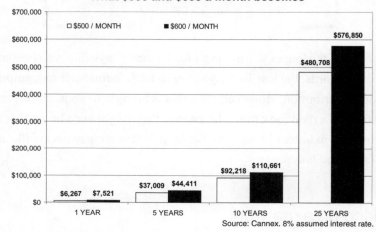

□ $500 / MONTH   ■ $600 / MONTH

	1 YEAR	5 YEARS	10 YEARS	25 YEARS
$500 / MONTH	$6,267	$37,009	$92,218	$480,708
$600 / MONTH	$7,521	$44,411	$110,661	$576,850

Source: Cannex. 8% assumed interest rate.

Let's be *really* optimistic and say that you could generate an extra $500 a month as a single or couple. If you put this money aside and earned 8 per cent on it, it would grow to $37,009 in just five years, $92,218 in 10 and $480,708 in 25.

But consider our cumulative total, assuming you can also save the same amount on your bills as Daniel and I did – $100. This would bring your total monthly saving to $600 and give you $44,411, $110,661 and $576,850 after five, 10 and 25 years respectively.

Not bad at all.

Top tips

> Monitor the salaries offered for jobs similar to yours in newspaper and internet advertisements or phone recruitment companies and ask about the pay rates in your field. If you discover you are under paid by comparison, bail up your boss (see page 29).

> As far as we've come with equal opportunity, women are still typically paid less for the same jobs as men. This is often because, while men will negotiate on price, women are much more likely to simply accept what is offered. Note to all females: ensure you are paid what you deserve in the first place and then do your utmost to see that your salary keeps pace with male colleagues, as well as the wider market.

Dirty tricks

> Promotions without pay rises.

Defence: Just say no. If they want you, let them prove it.

> While promotions often start immediately, it can take several weeks or even months to process pay increases. And not all employers will backdate them.

Defence: Stand your ground. However, if you look like losing all the back pay, propose a compromise date – it's better to get something than nothing.

Useful websites

Job sites:
www.mycareer.com.au,
www.seek.com.au
www.mycareer.com.au

Information on awards and industrial relations:
www.wagenet.gov.au (an Australian Government site).

Notes:

_____

_____

_____

_____

_____

_____

_____

_____

_____

_____

_____

_____

_____

_____

_____

_____

Step 4
Keep every cent you can

Years ago, I heard a quote from the model/actress/famous accessory Liz Hurley that really stuck in my mind. When asked how she managed to maintain her fabulous figure, she replied, "It's easy, you just have to want to be slim more than you want that piece of cheesecake, or that chocolate bar etc."

The reason the quote resonated with me so much was that you can apply exactly the same mentality to finance – it *is* easy, you just have to want to build your wealth more than you want those shoes, or that new couch etc.

I have a theory that any of us is capable of spending any amount of money. I distinctly remember getting my very first pay cheque from my $24,000 a year job as a cadet journalist – and wondering how I was ever going to spend all that cash! Guess what? I managed it, and have been managing it ever since.

Think about how much, after tax, you currently earn a year (if you don't know this figure, grab a calculator and multiply your after-tax weekly, fortnightly or monthly pay by 52, 26 or 12 respectively). Now, estimate how much you might have earned in your working life. What do you have to show for *all this money*?

If the answer is not much, there's a fair chance that you struggle to resist spending your whole pay packet. But here's the thing – anything you manage to save now, you *will* get to spend later. In fact, this will ensure there is something *left* to spend later. It's not about blanket denial but about deferred spending. And I would argue that you'll enjoy more what you work for, and look forward to, anyway.

What is it you want?

Unless you have very clear short, medium and long-term goals, you're unlikely to be motivated to save anything. Why wouldn't you instead spend everything you get when you get it?

So decide what you are saving for:

- In the shorter term, ie the next one to two years. For example, an overseas trip. We are currently saving for two holidays – a friend's wedding in Thailand next year and then a more expensive trip to visit family in England the following year. Another goal during this timeframe might be to pay off a credit card and/or a personal loan.

- In the medium term, ie the next three to five years. For instance, is your car going to need replacing within this period? If so, you should start planning to meet the expense (and remember from Step 2 the perils of borrowing for a depreciating asset). Or perhaps you would really like a new kitchen.

- In the longer term, ie five years and beyond. The ultimate goal – for all of us – should be to ensure that by the time we retire we have repaid at least our VBBD debts (to recap, those that are not tax deductible) and that our income will be adequate when we stop work. Remember, the 9 per cent of your salary that goes into your super fund is unlikely to be enough to sustain you for the whole of your retirement. So in this category you could include repay the mortgage and build a nice little nest egg.

With regards to your mortgage, the table on the next page shows how long it would take you to clear it if you paid 8 per cent interest, at various levels of overpayment (note how much you save in money and time by making even a small additional contribution).

You can calculate your precise 'debt freedom date' by jumping online and going to www.infochoice.com.au. Click 'home loans' on the left and then 'extra repayments' in the calculate section. Simply put in your loan details and the additional cash you are able to contribute and it will tell you when you could be debt free.

> Unless you have very clear short, medium and long-term goals, you're unlikely to be motivated to save anything

Saving in money and time from extra monthly repayments

	$50,000 loan	$100,000 loan	$150,000 loan	$200,000 loan	$250,000 loan	$300,000 loan	$350,000 loan	$400,000 loan	$450,000 loan	$500,000 loan
$100 extra	$31,074 / 10.5 yrs	$41,756 / 6.9 yrs	$47,360 / 5.1 yrs	$50,844 / 4.1 yrs	$53,234 / 4 yrs	$54,522 / 3 yrs	$55,843 / 2.5 yrs	$56,892 / 2.3 yrs	$57,749 / 2 yrs	$58,465 / 1.9 yrs
$200 extra	$41,578 / 14.4 yrs	$62,151 / 10.5 yrs	$74,832 / 8.3 yrs	$83,515 / 6.9 yrs	$89,864 / 5.9 yrs	$94,374 / 5.1 yrs	$98,192 / 4.5 yrs	$101,293 / 4.1 yrs	$103,865 / 3.7 yrs	$106,037 / 3.4 yrs
$300 extra	$47,077 / 16.7 yrs	$74,633 / 12.8 yrs	$93,229 / 10.5 yrs	$106,758 / 8.9 yrs	$117,096 / 7.7 yrs	$125,000 / 6.8 yrs	$131,617 / 6.1 yrs	$137,105 / 5.6 yrs	$141,737 / 5.1 yrs	$145,701 / 4.7 yrs
$400 extra	$50,496 / 18.1 yrs	$83,159 / 14 yrs	$106,554 / 12.1 yrs	$124,306 / 10.5 yrs	$138,307 / 9.2 yrs	$149,443 / 8.3 yrs	$158,835 / 7.5 yrs	$166,759 / 6.8 yrs	$173,541 / 6.3 yrs	$179,416 / 5.9 yrs
$500 extra	$52,837 / 19.1 yrs	$89,389 / 15.7 yrs	$116,712 / 13.4 yrs	$138,100 / 11.7 yrs	$155,383 / 10.5 yrs	$169,498 / 9.4 yrs	$181,525 / 8.6 yrs	$191,812 / 7.9 yrs	$200,722 / 7.4 yrs	$208,518 / 6.8 yrs
$600 extra	$54,545 / 19.8 yrs	$94,159 / 16.7 yrs	$124,740 / 14.4 yrs	$149,269 / 12.8 yrs	$169,475 / 11.5 yrs	$186,303 / 10.4 yrs	$200,787 / 9.6 yrs	$213,310 / 8.9 yrs	$224,278 / 8.3 yrs	$233,954 / 7.7 yrs
$700 extra	$55,846 / 20.4 yrs	$97,930 / 17.4 yrs	$131,261 / 15.3 yrs	$158,519 / 13.7 yrs	$181,331 / 12.4 yrs	$200,623 / 11.3 yrs	$217,380 / 10.5 yrs	$232,019 / 9.7 yrs	$244,931 / 9.1 yrs	$256,415 / 8.5 yrs
$800 extra	$56,872 / 20.9 yrs	$100,995 / 18.1 yrs	$136,671 / 16 yrs	$166,321 / 14.4 yrs	$191,462 / 13.2 yrs	$212,993 / 12.1 yrs	$231,849 / 11.2 yrs	$248,458 / 10.4 yrs	$263,215 / 9.8 yrs	$276,425 / 9.2 yrs
$900 extra	$57,702 / 21.2 yrs	$103,536 / 18.6 yrs	$141,237 / 16.7 yrs	$172,998 / 15.1 yrs	$200,230 / 13.8 yrs	$223,800 / 12.8 yrs	$244,593 / 11.9 yrs	$263,039 / 11.1 yrs	$279,535 / 10.5 yrs	$294,386 / 9.9 yrs
$1000 extra	$58,387 / 21.5 yrs	$105,678 / 19.1 yrs	$145,146 / 17.2 yrs	$178,782 / 15.9 yrs	$207,902 / 14.4 yrs	$233,333 / 13.4 yrs	$255,915 / 12.5 yrs	$276,076 / 11.7 yrs	$294,205 / 11.1 yrs	$310,612 / 10.5 yrs

Now you know how long that's going to take, grab a pen and calculator and list in the following table that and all your other personal goals for the money you earn. Write beside each one the date on which you would like to achieve it. Then put an estimate of what the goal will cost and how many pays there are until your target date – for example, if the target date is three years away and you are paid fortnightly, multiply 3 x 26 (the number of fortnights a year). Finally, divide the cost by the number of pays to find the amount you have to put aside each pay.

Short-term goals (1-2 years)

Goal	Target date	Cost	No. of pays	Savings per pay
Total		$		$

Medium-term goals (3-5 years)

Goal	Target date	Cost	No. of pays	Savings per pay
Total		$		$

Longer-term goals (5 years+)

Goal	Target date	Cost	No. of pays	Savings per pay
Total		$		$

The question is, can you afford all this?

Cashflow number crunch

It's time to look at your personal – or if you combine money with a partner, your household's – financial situation. This really comprises four elements – your income, your fixed costs, your discretionary spending and your saving. As you can simply look at your pay slips or bank accounts to see how much income you receive after tax each pay period, let's go straight to your fixed costs.

Putting aside for the big stuff

Your fixed costs are essential expenditure like repayments on borrowings, household bills, insurances, groceries and transport. This category of your personal financial statement also includes big *annual* expenses such as car registration and any annual insurance premiums. To prevent your finances from being derailed by a large bill such as these, treat them as you did the savings for your goals above and divide the cost by the number of pays. Jot down the figures in the next table, remembering we are only doing your annual bills at this stage.

Annual bills — required saving per pay

Bill	Cost	No. of pays a year	Savings per pay
Car insurance			
House and contents insurance			
Contents insurance			
Life insurance			
Income protection insurance			
Car registration			
Other			
Total	$		$

Arrange a direct debit of this amount into a dedicated bill bank account. I also try to throw in a bit extra for those expenses that are more difficult to predict like dental fees and car services. These are two areas you don't want to neglect as otherwise you might find yourself facing a huge outlay.

Naturally, it helps if your bills don't all arrive at once so your kitty doesn't come up short at any one point. Do what you can to spread them relatively evenly throughout the year.

What your upkeep costs

Now you know how much money you need to put aside for the 'big stuff', you can list your total fixed expenses each pay period. Transcribe into the next table your total savings required per pay from the table above, and then list any expenses that this *does not* cover. For bills that don't arrive as frequently as you are paid, simply figure out the number of pays you have to save for them and the amount you need to put aside from each pay, as above.

Regular expenses — amount per pay

Expense	Cost
Savings for annual bills (insert total from table on page 41)	
Groceries	
Mortgage/rent	
Credit card/s	
Personal loan/s	
Council rates	
Water rates	
Gas	
Electricity	
Body corporate	
Landline	
Mobile/s	
Internet	
Health insurance	
Petrol	
Public transport	
Child care	
School fees	
Car insurance	
House and contents insurance	
Contents insurance	
Life insurance	
Income protection insurance	
Car registration	
Other	
Total	$

As I touched on in Step 1, it's very possible to reduce even these so-called 'fixed' costs not just by shopping around for the best deal in the first place, but also by periodically checking that offerings haven't improved since. Being conservative in your use of water, electricity, or mobile phone etc also helps.

Although you might not realise it, you can probably also reduce your spend on groceries. I am a marketing manager's worst nightmare because I buy almost purely on price and have very little brand loyalty. Try purchasing only what is on sale one shopping trip and see what difference it makes at the checkout. Also, examine the items you actually buy – snacks in particular can work out very expensively, as can pre-prepared meals. Finally, it's a big mistake to go shopping when you are hungry – you'll spend more, and probably on items that are no good for your waistline. It's a little too much like torturing yourself anyway.

And, on the transport front, can you reduce your reliance on the car? If you have two, do you really need them?

Where you have total control

All that brings us to the moveable feast that is your discretionary spending. List on the table on the next page precisely where you spend the rest of your money. Try and think of everything and, when you are done, add 20 per cent to allow for what you've forgotten (do this by simply multiplying your total by 1.2).

Your discretionary spend each pay

Item	Spend
Gym membership	
Pay TV	
Work lunches	
Restaurants/bars	
Movies/concerts/theatre	
Alcohol	
Cigarettes	
Taxis	
Clothes	
Books/magazines	
Christmas saving	
Other gifts	
Other	
Total	$
Total x 1.2	$

Next, examine where you can trim the fat (yet another dietary analogy). For example:

- gym membership – could you exercise outside instead?
- pay TV – all those channels don't necessarily mean better viewing.
- lunches – it only takes five minutes to make your own and you would probably be healthier as a result.

With regards to entertainment, you could cut back on dinners and nights out by staying in with friends rather than going out. Similarly, alcohol and cigarettes can have a seriously detrimental effect on your future wealth. Smoking in particular is a money black hole – if you smoke a packet a day, you are spending no less than $70 a week. That's $3640 a year that you could be using instead to build your wealth.

Now I don't want to get all puritanical about this. I have to admit I would never cut out a glass or two of my favourite white wine, Verdelho. Just try to limit the frequency with which you indulge.

The more you manage to save, the more you will have to put towards your long-term goals.

Your bottom line

This is the moment of reckoning – in this final table, insert your income each pay period and take from it your fixed cost total and your discretionary spending total.

Your personal financial statement

After-tax income	
- Fixed costs	
- Discretionary spend	
Remaining money	$

If there is a negative figure, zero or only a small amount, go back to your previous lists and do more slashing. Remember, this is all going to go towards achieving your goals – so it will be worth it.

Now you know how much money you have to devote to achieve your goals. And the chances are there won't be enough. Which is why you need to prioritise them.

What to do with your cash

In the name of doubling your wealth, you should aim to put *at least* 50 per cent of the remaining money towards goals that are going to increase your net worth. That means if you carry over any credit card debt from month to month, have a personal loan or have a mortgage, these should be at the very top of your priority list. They should be in that order too, assuming the interest rate is highest on your credit card and lowest on your mortgage.

As I said earlier, any extra money you direct towards debts earns you a tax-free return equal to the interest rate you are paying. As far as wealth building goes, that takes some beating. Once you have paid all that off, you can start channelling your 50 per cent into investments. But we'll get into that shortly.

Next consider what else on your list of goals is important to you, and rank these things in priority order. You could either devote all your money to achieving that first thing, then once you have, move on to the second thing, etc. Or, alternatively, tackle a couple at a time – and split your money evenly between them (either keep good records of how much you've saved towards each, or do as we do and use a high-interest bank account that lets you operate several 'sub-accounts' under the same umbrella).

Much as I hate to say it, you may find you have to push back your target date for some of your goals. But don't despair, manage your money right and you *will* get there.

One final point – whatever it is that you choose to do with this remaining money, make sure you whisk it out of your bank account and into its destination as soon as you receive it. This is what financial experts mean when they say pay *yourself* first. Leave it in your working account and you are bound to simply spend it.

Here's a novel supplementary idea

As a means of generating even *more* money for what is really important to you, you could then try something else …

Every day we all make decisions with our discretionary spending that save money – but get no long-term benefit. Instead we promptly direct that saving into more consumption.

However, imagine how much you could achieve if you put each small saving you make *aside*. For example, if you buy a bottle of wine worth $10 rather than $15, put the $5 in a money jar. Same if you are really tempted to go out to dinner but take the more economical option of staying in – you've saved 40 odd dollars, so make that count by keeping it.

Save what you save and you will see an *immediate* and *identical* growth in your wealth. And nothing brings it home like squeezing the coins or notes into a money box.

Don't actually *leave* your money in a jar, though – put it onto your mortgage or into your wealth-building account as soon as possible so that it can start working for you.

And, if you are like me and hardly ever carry cash so don't have surplus actually in your wallet, make a note of how much you've saved, and transfer this amount to your wealth fund at the first possible opportunity, ensuring you don't pay fees every time you do this.

Just make sure you put every penny aside – in my best lecturing voice, you are only cheating yourself!

Wealth watch

What $200 and $800 a month becomes

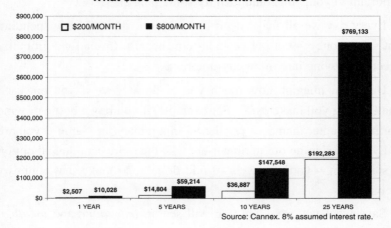

☐ $200/MONTH   ■ $800/MONTH

	1 YEAR	5 YEARS	10 YEARS	25 YEARS
$200/MONTH	$2,507	$14,804	$36,887	$192,283
$800/MONTH	$10,028	$59,214	$147,548	$769,133

Source: Cannex. 8% assumed interest rate.

Let's say, for example's sake, that by foregoing things or going cheaper during each month you manage to cut your outgoings by $200.

If you invested this money at 8 per cent, you would have $2507 after one year, $14,804 after five years, $36,887 after 10 years and $192,283 after 25.

But if you can also manage to cut $100 from your bills, as discussed in Step 1, and up your income by $500, as discussed in Step 3, you will amass a much more impressive $10,028 in one year, $59,214 in five years and $147,548 in 10 years.

However, it's the 25-year figure that is really phenomenal – $769,133. Wouldn't that be nice!

Top tips

> Further ways you could trim your costs include:

- o Shop at food and grocers' markets – the food is fresher and the prices are usually lower. To get the discounts on offer by buying in bulk, consider going in with friends.

- o Purchase something like The Entertainment Book, which offers discounts for restaurants (often 25 per cent off), movies, hotels and more. At a cost of $50-$60 a year, it should pay for itself very quickly. Also scour discount websites like www.lastminute.com.au to see what deals are on offer.

- o Drink cleanskins and premium cask wines – provided you are not a connoisseur, there are some very drinkable, and affordable, varieties.

- o Cooking can be cheaper than takeaway – but not always. Weigh up the comparative cost and try to go with what is more economical most of the time.

- o Buy fuel on Tuesdays, the day it is usually at its cheapest. And use the discounts from supermarket dockets wherever possible.

- o Shop for clothes and bigger items either at factory outlets or only when there are sales. But don't fall into the trap of buying more because it is cheaper. *Save* what you save.

- o Similarly, buy gifts in the sales and put them aside so they are on hand when each birthday rolls around.

- o When you are shopping for flights, there are a host of comparison websites (see page 51) that will find the best deals for you. These will charge if you book through them, but you don't have to.

- o Join a library. If you are big on books and magazines, this can save a fortune.

> If, for example, you should be able to pay off your mortgage in 12 years, really focus on this date – and count it down. That way, if you are tempted to reduce your overpayments one month, you will be acutely aware that this will push back the date on which you will be debt free.

> Keeping a picture of a desired holiday, bedroom setting or car will help your motivation to save for these goals. Every time you are tempted to spend money on something else, look at the picture and decide which you would rather have.

> If you find you are always running out of money well before your next pay, a big problem if you are paid monthly as we are, try eking it out over shorter periods. We have a holding account for the second fortnight's spending money that is called 'DO NOT TOUCH UNTIL THE 30TH!'. The name (together with the caps and exclamation mark) stops us from raiding it *most* of the time.

> Call your wealth-building account – whether savings or even a mortgage offset – something aspirational like the Early Retirement or Freedom Fund. The idea is to keep yourself focused on your chosen outcome.

> It's well worth making sure you can access at short notice a couple of thousand dollars of the money you have put aside for the future. While ideally you would leave this untouched, it can act as an emergency fund should you find yourself in a spot of bother – for example, if your car's engine blows up or if you unexpectedly need major dental work. You can't predict absolutely everything – and it's far preferable to have savings on hand than to go into debt.

> Take a leaf out of flamboyant British celebrity Quentin Crisp's book and focus only on your own assets and possessions. As he put it: "Never keep up with the Joneses. Drag them down to your level. It's cheaper."

Useful websites

Discount websites:
 www.entertainmentbook.com.au,
 www.lastminute.com.au,
 www.webjet.com.au,
 www.zuji.com.au
 www.flightcentre.com.au.

Notes:

_____

_____

_____

_____

_____

_____

_____

_____

_____

_____

_____

_____

_____

_____

_____

_____

_____

Step 5
Reward yourself

If you are feeling a little despondent about all that cost cutting in the previous Step, don't despair – this next section should cheer you up no end.

As I said right at the beginning of the book, you will *never* double your wealth if you deprive yourself of everything you enjoy that costs money. This is because you simply won't be able to keep it up. Sooner or later you will go on a spending spree, just as people who follow crazy diets sooner or later go on an eating binge (there's only so many grapefruits one person can handle).

I repeat, to be sustainable, wealth building has to be about moderation *not* deprivation.

With this in mind, you need to reward yourself. And the best way I have found of doing this is to take a cut of any 'bonus' money you get and to spend it in the most financially irresponsible way possible. An outrageously expensive pair of Manolo shoes. A visit to a barber that charges extortionate prices but gives you beer while having your hair cut. A cinema trip complete with the biggest bucket of popcorn they sell, a jumbo coke *and* a choc top ice-cream (although you'd need a fair bit of money to afford all that!). Splurge on whatever it is that takes your fancy.

Now, the bonus money I am talking about could come in several forms. It could actually be a bonus, it could be a tax refund, it could be a

small inheritance or it could be from some entirely random source. We once made more than $500 by agreeing to relinquish our tickets on an overbooked flight, then giving up our seats on the flight after that and the one after that. We were in Scotland, didn't have to be anywhere the next day – and were making £75 a pop.

However it comes, if you are fortunate enough to unexpectedly receive a lump sum, it is entirely acceptable to take some as your reward for containing your spending month in, month out. You have earned it.

No matter what the amount, I have 20 per cent earmarked as my cut. And, because the other 80 per cent goes towards building our long-term wealth, I don't have to waste a second feeling guilty. So from our $500 windfall from the airline, we took $100 and immediately spent it on clothes. Then we banked the rest.

I suggest you work to an 80:20 ratio as well. It gives you satisfaction on two levels – firstly, you get the thrill of unexpectedly having some money to fritter, and secondly, it brings you that much closer to doubling your wealth.

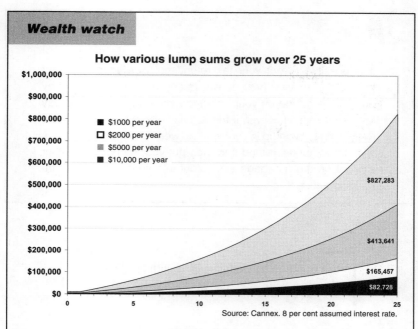

Wealth watch

How various lump sums grow over 25 years

Legend:
- ■ $1000 per year
- □ $2000 per year
- ▨ $5000 per year
- ■ $10,000 per year

$827,283

$413,641

$165,457

$82,728

Source: Cannex. 8 per cent assumed interest rate.

If you are able to put aside a lump sum of $1000 a year for 25 years, so $25,000 in total, you would have a really impressive lump sum of $82,728 if you invested it at 8 per cent.

But if you can find $2000 a year for the same period, $50,000 all up, you would have $165,457.

At $5000 a year, or $125,000 in total, you would have $413,641.

And on the off chance that you come across a $10,000 lump sum every year for 25 years, you would have $827,283. This is a spectacular $577,283 above the $250,000 you would have put in.

Remember too, that this is on top of any regular savings you have been able to make along the way.

> **Top tip:**

> It is possible to get your tax refund not in a lump sum, but throughout the year (you do what's called a variation). And by putting this refund on your mortgage immediately, you *will* pay less in interest. However, if these small bits of money are more likely to be sucked up in your week to week expenditure instead, stick to an annual refund and then put your 80 per cent either straight on the mortgage or straight into your chosen wealth-building account.

[
I repeat, to be sustainable, wealth building has
to be about moderation not deprivation.
]

Step 6
Invest smart

Now we come to the really fun part – deciding exactly how it is you will build your wealth.

As I have said already, when you consider the effective return, paying off your mortgage is one of the best 'investments' going – you earn a rate equal to the interest you pay *and* this is tax free. Beyond paying down debt, however, there is a world of assets and products you can consider.

It's also worth remembering that, even if your mortgage is your sole focus right now, your superannuation is quietly growing in the background thanks to the requirement for your employer to pay in 9 per cent of your salary. But it is up to you to decide where this is invested – although you have always been able to choose the *type* of fund, millions of Australian are now also able to choose the *manager* of that fund. So you really need to have some knowledge of investment.

The right investments for you will all depend on how long it is before you will need your money (or can *access* your money in the case of super) and your individual tolerance for risk – often referred to as the 'sleep at night' factor. Still have that pen handy? Then take my 'pillow test' to give you some indication of how much excitement you can take …

1. Is your main investment goal to:
   (a) Make impressive after-tax returns
   (b) Beat inflation with your returns
   (c) Have some protection against volatility
   (d) Preserve your capital

2. What would you do if an investment fell 20 per cent overnight?
   (a) Buy more as fast as I could
   (b) Shrug – they're long-term anyway
   (c) Cut some of my losses
   (d) Panic and sell the lot

3. How would you feel if an investment failed to deliver the expected return?
   (a) Ready for the next investment
   (b) Philosophical – it was always a risk
   (c) Pretty disappointed
   (d) Cheated

4. Do you mainly require:
   (a) Significant growth in your assets
   (b) Steady growth
   (c) Protection against volatility
   (d) Income

5. What annual return do you want and/or need?
   (a) More than 10 per cent
   (b) 9 to 10 per cent
   (c) 6 to 8 per cent
   (d) 5 per cent or below

6. How would you rate your investment knowledge?

    (a) Excellent

    (b) I'm pretty clued up

    (c) Not bad

    (d) What's investment?

7. What about your investment experience?

    (a) Extensive

    (b) Fairly wide

    (c) I've dabbled

    (d) What's investment?

8. How old are you?

    (a) 0-30

    (b) 31-45

    (c) 46-65

    (d) 66 or above

9. How long will you keep money invested?

    (a) More than 10 years

    (b) 6-10 years

    (c) 3-5 years

    (d) Less than three years

10. When do you intend to retire?

    (a) In 20 years or more

    (b) In 10-19 years

    (c) In 5-9 years

    (d) In 1-4 years

Your risk profile

Assign yourself a score of 4 for each (a) you circled, 3 for each (b), 2 for each (c) and 1 for each (d). Then tally up the numbers.

0-10 Conservative

Investments where there is little chance of losing money appeal most to you at this point in your life, despite their lower return potential.

Guide asset mix: Up to 30 per cent in growth assets such as shares and property and the rest in interest-bearing assets such as bonds and cash (see the risk continuum on page 62).

11-20 Moderate

Because you want some protection for your capital, you are prepared to accept more muted returns. Go for investments with potential for capital growth but also income if that growth doesn't eventuate.

Guide asset mix: Up to 50 per cent in growth assets and the rest in interest-bearing assets such as bonds and cash (see the risk continuum on page 62).

21-30 Entrepreneurial

You place more importance on long-term capital growth than on short-term volatility. Income is not likely to be an investment priority at this stage.

Guide asset mix: Up to 70 per cent in growth assets and the rest in interest-bearing assets such as bonds and cash (see the risk continuum on pge 62).

31-40 Aggressive

You are seeking after-tax returns that far outstrip inflation and are willing to take a fair amount of risk, and accept the volatility that brings, to get them.

Guide asset mix: Up to 85 per cent in growth assets and the rest in interest-bearing assets such as bonds and cash (see the risk continuum on page 62).

Other considerations

Of course, thorough risk profiling is rather more complex than that little exercise suggests. In fact, there is an entire academic discipline – psychometrics – dedicated to such psychological testing.

But you should bear in mind that in most risk questionnaires people come out more risk averse than they can afford to. Yes, you need to be able to sleep at night, but you also need to achieve your investment objectives. Although a risk-free return of 5 per cent a year might sound appealing, it won't be much good if you actually need 8 per cent to be able to retire when you would like.

So you have to balance psychology with necessity.

In a nutshell, if you are investing for the long term, you will need more exposure to growth assets; if you are investing for the short term, you will need more exposure to interest-bearing and other safer assets.

Your basic options

The below risk/reward continuum provides a snapshot of the different investment options, and the returns you can expect from them.

LOW RISK

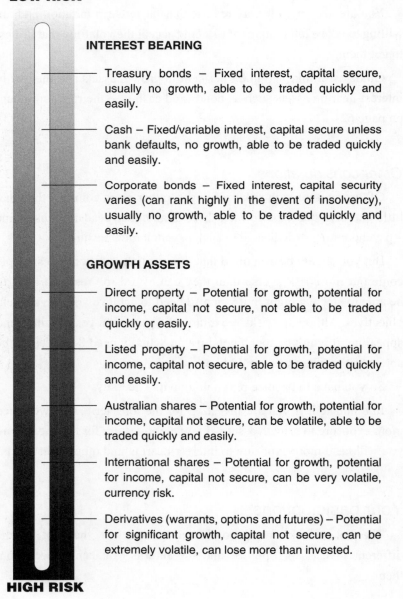

INTEREST BEARING

Treasury bonds – Fixed interest, capital secure, usually no growth, able to be traded quickly and easily.

Cash – Fixed/variable interest, capital secure unless bank defaults, no growth, able to be traded quickly and easily.

Corporate bonds – Fixed interest, capital security varies (can rank highly in the event of insolvency), usually no growth, able to be traded quickly and easily.

GROWTH ASSETS

Direct property – Potential for growth, potential for income, capital not secure, not able to be traded quickly or easily.

Listed property – Potential for growth, potential for income, capital not secure, able to be traded quickly and easily.

Australian shares – Potential for growth, potential for income, capital not secure, can be volatile, able to be traded quickly and easily.

International shares – Potential for growth, potential for income, capital not secure, can be very volatile, currency risk.

Derivatives (warrants, options and futures) – Potential for significant growth, capital not secure, can be extremely volatile, can lose more than invested.

HIGH RISK

Diversification

The age-old saying 'never put all your eggs in one basket' goes to the heart of diversification – spread your risk and you have much less chance of losing money.

But you also have much less chance of making a lot of money. The higher-risk alternative is to spread your money across a smaller selection of well-researched assets in the hopes of *making* a 'killing'. As American author Mark Twain put it: "Put all your eggs in the one basket and watch that basket."

However, I wouldn't recommend the second approach unless you have an extremely high 'sleep at night' threshold – and you are very, very knowledgeable.

To be truly diversified you need to spread your investments across a range of different asset classes, such as cash, bonds, property and shares. Think about whether they are *really* spread too – if you have a home, an investment property or two, and a bunch of cash in mortgages trusts (more about these in Step 8), you really hold only one type of asset – property. So you are vulnerable to a cyclical downturn in that asset class.

But you should also invest in different sectors within each asset class – for example, a spread of shares including resource, banking and say, technology stocks, and not just residential but also commercial property.

Finally, you need to consider the geographical bias in your portfolio.

Australia represents only 2 per cent of the world's market. Besides, if every one of your assets is in the one country, you are incredibly exposed to a local economic downturn. (It is easiest to achieve geographic diversification by investing in managed funds that invest internationally, which we'll get to in the next section).

Don't fall into the very common trap of believing that you have a diversified portfolio when it is anything but.

> Spread your risk and you have much less chance of losing money. But you also have much less chance of **making** a lot of money

Direct or indirect

With most of the above investments, you have two basic options. The first is to purchase them direct – so, for example, you would purchase individual bonds from the issuing company or through the stock market, a property from a vendor or shares, again, via the stock market.

Alternatively, you could pool your money with that of other investors and purchase these investments through what are known as managed funds. Available for just about every asset class, because of the sheer size of these funds, you are able to achieve far greater diversification than you would be able to with only your own money.

The advantage of direct investing is that there are no management fees. But, naturally, that means you have to make your own trading decisions (unless you use a full-service, more expensive broker). With indirect – or managed fund – investing, you pay an expert a percentage of your investment to make the trading decisions for you.

More than 80 per cent of Australians have their super in a 'balanced' managed fund. This type of fund holds up to about 70 per cent in growth assets such as shares and property and the rest in bonds, cash and possibly a few other asset classes. With such a spread of investments, the idea is that the returns will be fairly consistent year after year.

For younger people, however, it can be a better idea to invest in funds that hold a higher proportion of growth assets as these are the assets that, although risky in the short term, make higher returns over the long term. It is also possible to cut human error out of the equation by investing in funds that are not run by managers at all but are simply made up of the shares that comprise a market index, in the same proportions as that index. The idea of these so-called index funds is to simply replicate the market's performance. And their big advantage is that they are very cheap.

Frankly stunning

Now let's take a closer look at one of the most popular investments – shares (also referred to as stocks).

A share is quite literally a share in a company, which is why it is also called equity. The alternative is debt, the category bonds fall into. Here you lend money to a government or company at a given interest rate, usually for a particular period of time, for it to use as it sees fit.

Equities offer the potential for not just growth or capital gain, but also for income in the form of dividends. Dividends represent a share in the profits a company makes and are usually paid twice yearly. Many companies offer a facility to reinvest these dividends into more shares, sometimes at a discounted price, without having to pay any trading fee (more on that in just a minute).

> Yes, you need to sleep at night, but you also
> need to achieve your investment objectives

But the real beauty of dividends is that they come with what are known as franking credits – credits for tax the company has already paid on its profits. Because this is levied at 30 per cent, dividends are effectively tax free in the hands of 30 per cent taxpayers. And 47 per cent taxpayers pay only the difference with the 30 per cent company rate, 17 per cent. But taxpayers on the 15 per cent rate and below actually get a *refund* of the additional tax the company has paid. (To keep things simple, tax rates here ignore the 1.5 per cent Medicare levy). Very nice indeed.

All this only applies if a dividend is fully franked, however. It can also be partially or even 'un'-franked, which would mean paying tax on it at your marginal rate. For this reason, many investors choose only to invest in shares with a fully-franked dividend. It's also worth remembering that when you take franking credits into account, the income you can earn from bank **shares** is often higher than you can earn from having your money in a standard bank *deposit* account.

How to trade

If you want to invest direct, the best idea is to open an online savings account paying a high rate of interest and to save into it. Once you have amassed $2500, buy your first parcel of shares. Then every time your account subsequently reaches $2500, buy another parcel. Not only are you keeping your exposure relatively small by doing this, but you are not sinking all your money into the market at the same time so are protected against a market slump.

The good news is that the actual cost of trading has never been cheaper thanks to the proliferation of online brokers. With more than a dozen now competing for your business, including CommSec (www.comsec.com.au), E*Trade (www.etrade.com.au), National Online (www.tradingonline.com.au) and Westpac Broking (broking.westpac.com.au), you can buy or sell a small parcel of shares for less than $20 (but bear in mind you have to trade a few times a year to qualify for this price. For a one-off trade, expect to pay around $50). Registration is free, so it's worth joining a couple and seeing which website you like the best.

To begin trading you will need to download an application form, which basically asks you to verify your identity and fill in your bank details. Some brokers also require you to open a linked bank account with a particular institution, while others don't make this compulsory but will charge you less per trade if you do. If the interest rate on this account is less than you can get in a separate online account, then move your money across only when you are ready to buy.

A few days after posting in your application form, you will receive your ID number, at which point you are ready to trade. The only other thing you need to know is that there is no longer any stamp duty on share transactions (something shares have over property) and your trading costs are tax deductible after you sell.

Where to find information

Of course, the tricky part is deciding which shares to buy. Here, you have two main options – a top-down approach or a bottom-up approach.

Top down would be to identify a particular sector that might be about to benefit due to changing economic, political or demographic conditions. As an example, you might take the view that the aged care sector is about to surge because of the ageing population. You would then look at the individual stocks within that sector (you can find what these are by looking at the *Weekend Australian Financial Review*'s share list) and decide which you think have the best prospect of success.

The bottom-up approach, on the other hand, would be to identify a particular company that might have a good chance of growing its business. This doesn't require any specialist investment knowledge at all – it can just be via observation in your day-to-day travels. In other words, just activate your inbuilt investment radar. For example, perhaps there is a new product at the supermarket that everyone has suddenly started talking about. Or maybe you've noticed that a particular restaurant chain now has queues out the door most nights. You are just as equipped as a market expert to identify the companies with a winning formula.

Once you have, the next step is to read widely about the company (or companies) in a bid to determine whether it might be a good investment. What you are looking for is companies that are undervalued by the market but whose underlying business is sound. You can glean this information by regularly reading *The Australian Financial Review,* the *AFR Smart Investor* magazine, the business and personal finance sections of newspapers and other specialist investment magazines. Many online brokers also offer a host of free information and features to help you make your trading decisions.

Investor psychology

The psychology of investing is a fascinating thing. On the one hand, rather than cutting our losses and subjecting ourselves to the regret that will bring, we convince ourselves we just haven't given the investment enough time. On the other hand, rather than locking in a decent level of profit from a surging investment, greed can cause us to hold too long and lose the chance. Fear plays a part here, too: the fear of missing out on future gains.

All of which is precisely why you should base your investment decisions not on emotions but on maths. When trading in shares in particular, implement what's called a trailing stop loss. Very simply, if a share falls a pre-determined percentage – say, 10 per cent – below its highest price, you sell. To calculate this trigger price, just divide the highest price by 10 and then deduct that figure from it. For example, if a share has just reached $20 you would take away $2 (20 ÷ 10), to give you a lowest acceptable price of $18.

Similarly, decide on a level of profit with which you are happy, whether it be 20, 30 or 40 per cent and, if you achieve it, walk away satisfied. You can calculate this figure by multiplying the purchase price by 1.2, 1.3 or 1.4 respectively.

Some online brokers allow you to set what's called a 'conditional order' to automatically sell if a share's price reaches either your stop loss or your desired profit level.

> Fear plays a part here, too:
> the fear of missing out on future gains

Wealth watch

Would you swap your house for a few tulips? What about those few acres on the coast? You don't use them anyway and the tulips really are exquisite …

In Holland in the 1600s people did. One man reportedly offered nearly five hectares of land for just one tulip bulb, such was the belief that the flower could generate big money. It was a classic mania that has come to embody the dangers of all manias or bubbles – floral or otherwise.

Many Dutch lost everything when the market – as markets always do when they have spiralled that far out of control – crashed. Well, not quite everything I suppose. They had a tulip or two (if they had been very wealthy!).

There have been manias here too. Think the Poseidon Boom. Dotcoms. And property.

All of the above provide an example of herd psychology, which, bubble or no bubble, can hurt your investment returns.

In fact, one investment theory goes that you should do the very opposite of what everyone else is doing and become a 'contrarian' investor.

So rather than buying tech stocks when they were 'licences to print money', you should have been sticking with the boring old economy stocks. (It ultimately worked for investment guru Warren Buffett, who shunned dotcom stocks on the basis that they had little intrinsic value.)

And, as opposed to queuing with the throngs waiting to inspect yet another property in the hopes that this time they will secure one, you should have found a comfortable vantage point, grabbed a coffee and laughed at them.

It's well acknowledged that it's impossible to pick the peaks and troughs of markets. However, they are driven by sentiment and by going against that you have a much better shot at buying at the bottom and selling at the top, the investment Holy Grail. Follow the herd and you're more likely to do the opposite.

Borrowing to invest

When most people think about borrowing to invest, they think about property. But you can just as easily borrow to invest in shares and managed funds. One way of doing this is to borrow against the equity in your house by taking out something like a home equity loan, while another is to open a dedicated margin loan facility, which is usually secured not against your house but against a share portfolio.

Just like when you borrow to invest in property, you are able to claim your interest and costs as tax deductions. However, if you borrow to buy fully-franked shares the tax benefits are greater than the tax benefits of borrowing to buy property.

'Gearing up' like this magnifies both your gains and your losses. For this reason, most people tend to borrow no more than 50 per cent of the value of their investment. The biggest risk with a margin loan is that if your shares fall in value, the lender may require you to repay some of the loan by using either cash or by selling some shares. This is known as a margin call.

Most financial institutions will lend money for a share portfolio. They should also be able to provide you with scenarios to show you how to keep your gearing to an acceptable level. Just bear in mind that the strategy will only prove profitable if your after-tax gain is greater than your costs, including interest.

> The psychology of investing is a fascinating thing

Top tips

> If you are considering investing in growth assets such as shares and property, you should be prepared to keep them for at least five years. These investments can be volatile over the shorter term but historically outperform over longer terms.

> For any money you can't afford to lose, stick to capital-protected investments such as online savings accounts and bonds bought at issue (so directly from governments or companies) that you are prepared to hold until the named redemption date.

> On that point, however, there are bonds and there are bonds. If the issuing government or company goes bust, you are unlikely to get your money back. To get an indication of which bonds are high risk, refer to the Standard & Poors credit rating – any bond rated 'BBB', 'A', 'AA' or 'AAA' (the highest rating) is considered investment grade and therefore carries a lower risk of default. Invest in anything rated below that and you stand a greater chance of losing your money (but you will be paid more in interest as a result).

> Be aware that, when investing internationally, changes in exchange rates could affect your return. If the Aussie dollar goes up against the currency in which you have invested, you will lose money. However, if it falls, you will make money. Some fund managers 'hedge' against this risk, which means they buy derivatives to ensure it is investment performance alone that determines your returns. Such funds are a safer way to invest overseas. Unless you are prepared to take on this additional risk, check before handing over your cash.

> Don't understand an investment? Maybe you're not meant to. Don't invest in it.

Dirty tricks

> If someone comes up to you with a wink and a nudge and gives you a hot investment tip, it could be that they have an ulterior motive. If the tip is so good, why are they sharing it? Do they stand to gain in any way?

Defence: Either ignore them or do your own research and invest an amount you can afford to lose. Remember that no one, no matter how expert, cares about protecting and growing your money as much as you do.

Useful websites

Online brokers:
www.comsec.com.au, www.etrade.com.au, www.trading.national.com.au and broking.westpac.com.au

Managed fund information:
www.morningstar.com.au and www.ifsa.com.au

Super information:
www.asfa.asn.au
(Association of Superannuation Funds of Australia).

Company information:
www.afr.com.au and www.asx.com.au

Shareholder information:
www.asa.asn.au (Australian Shareholders' Association).

Investor education:
www.asx.com.au

Bond ratings information:
www.standardandpoors.com.au

Notes:

_____

_____

_____

_____

_____

_____

_____

_____

_____

_____

_____

_____

_____

_____

_____

_____

_____

_____

_____

Step 7
Use the system to help rather than hinder you

Unfortunately, your finances don't exist in a vacuum – fees and taxes diminish your wealth, so you need to do all you can to minimise both. Here are a few brief pointers.

Fees

Either opt for financial products with low fees or be sure that higher fees result in better investment performance. You can find this out by checking historic returns, but remember that good *past* performance doesn't necessarily translate into good *future* performance. In fact, the year after a managed fund tops its sector, it usually slumps to way down in the middle of the pack. This is precisely why you need to look beyond one-year performance to three-, five- and even 10-year performance when choosing an investment.

With regards to bank accounts, structure these so that you pay as little in fees as possible. You can either choose a working account that allows only a limited number of free transactions but has no monthly fee, or an account that allows unlimited free transactions, for a monthly fee of about $5. It will all depend on how often you withdraw money or pay for things on a card.

It may also be worth examining your banking habits to see whether you could cut down on transactions and therefore pay less in fees. The very best way of doing this is to double up – when you use eftpos,

which is one of the cheapest ways to access money at around 60 cents a pop (when you are out of free transactions), also withdraw cash. That way you are getting two transactions for the price of one. With just a little forward thinking, it's possible you could get away with having an account with only a few free transactions – and avoid a monthly fee altogether. Incidentally, the hands-down most *expensive* way of accessing cash is to withdraw it from a credit card. Cash withdrawals come with a fee of about 1.5 per cent, even if you are in credit. So, if you take out $200, it could cost you $3.

When you are not accessing your own but the bank's money, you also incur a higher than normal rate of interest from day one.

Don't let penalties undo all your hard work, though. Miss a credit card payment, accidentally go into the red or have a direct debit dishonoured and you could be up for as much as $50. Automatic transfers will take the onus off you and ensure you don't make a costly mistake. But if your bank has the dubious policy of charging you an overdrawn fee when it is one of *its* fees that has put you into the red, kick up a big stink. This is plain rude and if they don't refund the money, I would suggest taking your business elsewhere.

Taxes

Taxes are one area where it's vital to know how to work the system – or to secure the services of a good accountant to tell you how.

At the most basic, you need to ensure you claim every possible tax deduction, as these are yours by rights and could earn you a refund. Pay particular attention to any geared investments, where it can be easy to miss a deduction or two.

If you are single and earn more than $50,000 a year or part of a couple that earns more than $100,000 a year, it is a no-brainer to buy private medical insurance. If you don't, you will have to pay the Medicare surcharge on top of the Medicare levy. You don't have to buy top of the line cover though – basic hospital cover suffices. We will look at the importance of protecting your health and earning power in Step 9.

Beyond this, there are strategies you can put in place to minimise the tax you pay. For example, you can take advantage of the independent taxation of married couples by putting any assets you own *outright* in the name of the lower-paid spouse, so that any income or eventual capital gain is taxed at a lower rate. However, investments for which there are *borrowings* should generally be in the name of the higher rate taxpayer, so that they attract the maximum deductions for costs.

You could also consider salary packaging, which means taking benefits such as a company car, a laptop or even super contributions (see next page for more on this) in place of some of your wages. The idea is that, rather than pay for these items out of post-tax salary, you use pre-tax salary and therefore increase your disposable income. Just watch that you are not caught by fringe benefits tax – at 48.5 per cent, this would cost more than income tax for all but those in the highest tax bracket. It's a complex area and, if you are considering packaging anything but super, I recommend seeing a licensed adviser first.

> Taxes are one area where it's vital to know how
> to work the system

Finally, people with a spouse on a low income can earn a generous rebate by making a contribution to their super scheme. Which leads us nicely into the next topic ...

Super

There are some fantastic opportunities to maximise your wealth by working the superannuation system.

One of the biggest government giveaways is the superannuation co-contribution. This refers to the fact that people who earn less than $28,000 a year and contribute $1000 after tax to their super fund receive a contribution of $1500 from the government. An instant 150 per cent return is simply phenomenal. Even better, the co-contribution *phases out* beyond $28,000 and people earning up to $58,000 receive a partial benefit.

Earlier we touched on salary packaging. Well, you can use this to become eligible for such benefits as the co-contribution. And if you salary sacrifice into super, you win on several fronts. Here's how you can work it:

Say you are a higher rate taxpayer. Anything you salary sacrifice into super will be taxed not at 48.5 per cent but at only 15 per cent, the rate at which super contributions are taxed. But if you sacrifice yourself down to a lower tax bracket, 43.5 per cent or even 31.5 percent, you will save more again. Finally, if your salary is now below $58,000 and you contribute $1000 to super *after* tax, you will also receive a partial co-contribution. The strategy works for everyone above the 16.5 per cent tax bracket, though the tax saving will be less.

Wealth watch

CHANCES are you put your spare money – well, the spare money you resist spending – onto your mortgage. After all, owning your home outright is a fundamental step in building your wealth.

But it's just possible that you could make more of this money by directing it straight into your super fund. Here's why.

As I explained earlier, by making extra mortgage repayments, you are effectively getting a return equal to your mortgage interest rate. What's more, this return is tax-free.

However, you have already paid tax on that money through the pay-as-you-go system.

If, instead, you arranged a salary sacrifice into your super fund, that same amount of money becomes a significantly higher contribution because such contributions come from pre-tax money. They are reduced only by the 15 per cent contributions tax. Provided this is less than your rate of income tax, you are immediately ahead.

Of course, your rate of return will determine how this ultimately pans out for you. But even if the growth of your super fund falls short of the interest rate on your mortgage, it will take years to make up for that initial contributions boost.

Let's assume you earn $60,000 a year and have $5000 of gross salary to put towards either your mortgage or your super. If you go the mortgage option, in the 2005/2006 financial year you would have $3425 left after tax to put in. If you go the super option, your $5000 would become a $4250 contribution.

So you start way out in front with super.

But where will you be in 20 years if the average standard variable rate is 7.25 per cent and the average annual super fund return is 7.5 per cent (after fees and taxes)?

Assuming 4 per cent wages inflation, Rice Walker Actuaries says you would have $31,975 more in super (after tax) than you would have paid off your mortgage ($194,047 versus $162,072).

> The outperformance of super over the mortgage increases for incomes above $60,000 and decreases for incomes below it. Only on a salary of less than $21,100 is it better to pay off your mortgage.
>
> Of course, the variables, being variables, could change. Interest rates could rise; super returns could fall. On current rates, your fund needs to earn at least 5.6 per cent a year for you to be better off in super. But if mortgage interest rates increased by 1 percentage point, you would need to earn 6.7 per cent.
>
> However, the strategy has one big flaw – you have to wait until you are at least 55 to access your super (the age is already 60 for those born after 1965). If there is a chance you will need the money before then, it's not the way to go.

A fallback plan

In some ways, putting money into super – particularly if you are quite young – is a leap of faith. Governments are bound to change the rules over and over throughout the decades – and who knows what the age at which you can access it will be in 20 or 30 years' time.

Which is why it may pay to also save into a separate, growth-based investment (such as a share portfolio or a selection of managed funds) designated specifically for retirement. You could even aim to use this fund to retire early, drawing down on it until the government will let you have your super (assuming you will have enough in super when your early retirement nest egg runs out).

When finally you can access your super, also consider taking the allowable tax-free lump sum and investing it in non-super growth investments for the next 25 years or so. This way if your retirement income stream runs out, which they quite often do, you will have a back-up lump sum on which to live. And if you die before then, it can be your legacy to your kids.

Top tips

> There is more than $7bn in super listed on the Australian Taxation Office's 'lost members register'. If you have changed jobs or moved without telling your super fund, the chances are some of it is yours. To find out, go to the ATO website, www.ato.gov.au, look under 'superannuation', and then click 'find your lost super'. It's a simple matter of typing in your tax file number and a few other details about yourself. Once you have found any lost funds, think about consolidating them into the one fund to cut down on fees.

> When you marry or have children, it is important to make a will. Otherwise, if you die, your assets will be distributed according to a legal formula that may mean they won't go to the people you would want. What's more, they won't go *anywhere* quickly – if you die without a will, or 'intestate', the distribution of your assets can take years. You can make a will at the Public Trustee for free, although you may need to appoint it as 'executor', for which there is a charge. However, this might be preferable to appointing a friend or family member as there can be a massive amount of work involved.

> It is also worth making a 'binding death nomination' for the money that's in your super fund. If you don't, this will probably be paid directly into your estate to be distributed as per your will. The problem with this is that it may mean big delays and heavy fees and taxes. Ask your super fund for the form.

> Consider also giving enduring power of attorney to a spouse and/ or adult child. This means that, should you lose mental capacity, they would have the authority to manage your financial affairs. The worst case scenario if you don't is frozen bank accounts and your family left high and dry. You can find the appropriate form at most newsagents or, alternatively, engage a solicitor to draw up a document.

> Sometimes using the system to help you is not all it's cracked up to be – and the Pensioner Concession Card is a case that

springs to mind. Many retires do whatever it takes to reduce their assets or income so that they qualify for the card, which entitles you to cheaper prescriptions, travel and car registration, and discounts on utilities bills, among other things. 'Whatever it takes' usually entails spending money until they are below the threshold, giving money away (although there are restrictions here) or locking it up in investments that are partially exempt from the assets test. However, before you go doing this, you really need to do your sums to make sure you are getting more than you are giving up – you might have to sacrifice thousands in annual income to receive only several hundreds of dollars of benefits. You could well be better off without it.

Dirty tricks

> You are probably aware that you need to hold an investment for one year to qualify for the 50 per cent reduction in capital gains tax. But, technically speaking, you actually need to hold it for one year and two days – there must be one *clear* year between the day you make the contract to buy the investment and the day you make the contract to sell it.

Defence: Wait the full *367* days if you want to qualify for the reduction. Many people have faced an unexpected bill due to this wrinkle. Incidentally, if you are able to wait until you retire to sell, this would mean a lower capital gains tax bill. And, provided you sell within two years of finishing work, you may even be able to reduce this further by making a tax-deductible contribution to super.

> Again on capital gains tax, if two people who each own their own houses get married, they have a couple of options. One, they can nominate the same house as their main residence and rent out the other property, at which point capital gains tax starts accruing on it. Two, they can nominate *both* houses as main residences, and receive only a 50 per cent exemption on each

from the date they move in together. In other words, the six-year grace period that would normally apply when you move out of a home does not.

Defence: Either sell one property before (or shortly after) the marriage – or prepare to pay some tax!

Useful websites

Wills:
www.publictrustee.com.au
(the Government body responsible for making wills).

Pension Concession Card and benefits information:
www.centrelink.gov.au and www.ato.gov.au

Tax information:
www.ato.gov.au

Super information:
www.asfa.asn.au
(Association of Superannuation Funds of Australia) and
www.apra.gov.au
(Australian Prudential Regulation Authority).

Notes:

Step 8
Don't let anyone sabotage you

We all want to believe there is a short-cut to building wealth. And, if you get in just before a boom, you certainly can make a lot of money quickly (assuming, that is, that you sell before any bust).

But ordinarily wealth accumulation is a slow steady process. If you expect as much, you are much less likely to be seduced by the promise of a quick buck.

Every year the Australian Securities and Investments Commission issues what it calls the Pie in the Sky Award. This award goes to the investment scheme with the most ludicrous, unsubstantiated promises of returns. Here is a sample of past winners:

> An 'interest-free' loan – 240 people invested in a scheme that involved purchasing a car through a car buyers' club, borrowing a little more from their financier and then investing this excess offshore. The idea was that high returns from the offshore investment would repay their car loans. As you will have predicted, this investment failed to deliver and people were left to fund their own repayments. Unfortunately, because they believed they wouldn't have to meet this cost themselves, many had borrowed more than they could afford.

> Early access to your super – why wait until you retire to get at your super if you can access it now? This scheme was complex but basically involved setting up a self-managed super fund, investing offshore, and getting a cheap loan from your own fund. The reality is that such schemes are illegal and can involve heavy penalties, including tax penalties.

> Swap your worthless dotcom shares for blue-chip stocks (shares in Australia's largest companies) – this one was pretty straightforward. After sucking investors in with a cold call, they hit them for 'fees'. Needless to say, the blue chips never arrived.

Nothing will serve you better in your quest to build wealth than healthy scepticism – if it seems too good to be true, the promoter is probably lying. Run a mile.

The easiest way to recognise either a dodgy financial product or a higher-risk financial product is a headline rate of return above what you can get, for example, from an online savings account. The more a product offers beyond this, the more risk is involved. Be very wary indeed.

Identity fraud

Beyond get-rich-quick schemes, you also need to take every step you can to protect yourself from identity fraud. Here are four of the most common scams:

Phishing

The term phishing refers to the process of trying to obtain personal details by sending a fake email from a bank. This email will ask for information including pin numbers, online banking passwords and credit card expiry dates. Of course, once fraudsters have these they can

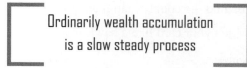

Ordinarily wealth accumulation
is a slow steady process

clean you out. You may even be rerouted back into the legitimate bank website so you are unaware what has happened.

No matter how authentic an email looks, remember that banks will *never* ask you for such details over email. Hit delete!

Cloning

This is a form of identity fraud I know something about – I have had my credit card 'cloned' or 'skimmed' not once but three times.

As you will have guessed, the term refers to card copying. It is easily done – a fraudster simply swipes your card through a second machine when you hand it over to pay. This machine creates a magnetic strip identical to the one on the back of your card, which holds all your details. This is then attached to a new card with a different name on it, signed by the fraudster and put to use.

While financial institutions have finally realised they need to invest the money to protect against this type of fraud, I am sorry to say there is little you can do to guard against it in the meantime. I distinctly remember the bank representative, when I reported the first batch of unauthorised transactions on my card, asking me if I ever had let it out of my sight. "All the time," I replied. "At every restaurant and every bar." It's incredibly difficult not to.

But it turns out the card was copied not in one of these 'high risk' situations but at my local convenience store – when I was standing *right there*. The card machine was under the counter out of site, apparently just beside the copying machine. Another common trick is to pretend to drop your card behind the counter and then quickly swipe it.

If you can, watch your card like a hawk.

Nigerian letter scam

This scam has been around *forever* – and manifests itself in many different ways. The most common approach is to send you an email purporting to be from a Nigerian dignitary who needs to get money out of the country. The email asks if it would be ok to deposit the money in your bank account in return for a cut. Of course, for that your bank details are necessary – and you can bet that far from going up, your bank balance will go down.

However, I have seen many other stories used in conjunction with this same scam. One of the most notable emanates from Iraq, and asks for help for Saddam Hussein's little-known son, Nassery. Under this incarnation, you are promised 20 per cent for helping him get his loot out, but need to pay some 'fees' in advance.

It's pretty safe to assume that anyone who emails you out of the blue and asks to put money in your account is trying to do the very opposite. Hit delete!

Rummaging though the bin

Unless you tear up all credit card slips or bank statements, you are leaving yourself open to identity fraud. For fraudsters, the pay off for spending just a few minutes going through your bin – or even an unlocked mailbox – can be significant. With your credit card numbers in their possession, they simply need to get on the phone or jump online to make purchases.

Investing in a shredder could pay for itself over and over.

Wealth watch

The Australian Securities and Investments Commission offers the following tips to stop yourself becoming a victim of fraud:

1. Keep your credit cards safe.

2. Choose hard-to-guess PINs and passwords. This rules out your date of birth, part of your name or address, or your partner's name or address because, if thieves steal your bag, they could easily guess these passwords.

3. Passwords should be kept secret and strictly to yourself.

4. If you write down any PINs or passwords, not only disguise them but be sure to also keep the piece of paper in a different place from your credit cards. Similarly, if you use the card to make online purchases, don't store internet banking passwords on your computer in an undisguised form. Send your card details only through secure internet sites, which you will recognise by the web preface 'https//:'. The 's' stands for secure server. Secure sites will also have a padlock in the bottom right-hand corner of the screen.

5. While we're on the topic of padlocks, secure your letterbox with one.

6. Carefully check your bank statements (this will help you keep track of where you are spending your money too). If there are any purchases that aren't yours, contact your financial institution immediately so you stand the best chance of getting the money back.

7. Along those same lines, tell your institution as soon as you realise that your card has been stolen or lost. And finally;

8. Make sure your financial provider always knows your current contact details so it can contact you in the event of any irregular card activity.

Top tips

> Before signing up with any scheme promising big returns, log on to www.asic.gov.au and check whether the company holds an Australian Financial Services licence (just click on the financial services homepage on the left and then 'searching our databases' in the middle). It is also a really good idea to type the company's name into the site's search engine to see what comes up. Finally, get the Product Disclosure Statement and read *every* word.

> Be wary of salespeople who make grand promises they can't back up, those who don't give you a detailed account of the risks and anyone who tries to pressure you into signing your money over. It really is buyer beware when it comes to financial products so do your research thoroughly.

Dirty tricks

> All of the scams mentioned earlier.

Defence: Vigilantly guard against them.

> There is a new scam where someone calls you to say there has been suspicious activity on your credit card, asks you if you made a particular purchase and then requests the three-digit security number from the back of your card.

Defence: If someone calls purporting to be from a bank, don't give them *any* of your card details. Instead, ask for a name and contact number and then call your bank to check they are legit.

> You can't open a newspaper without finding an ad for interest-bearing investment products that at first glance just look like very attractive term deposits. They are actually nothing like them because there is risk to your capital. Sometimes advertised under the titles 'mortgage trusts' or 'mortgage funds', if you invest you are essentially lending money to the issuer for a certain period,

for a fixed or variable rate of interest. Most often, they will in turn lend your money for mortgages over residential and commercial properties, and to property developers.

There are two main types – debentures and unsecured notes. With debentures, your investment should be secured over the assets (the properties the fund lends against). But with unsecured notes, it is only secured by the *loans* over the assets. This latter incarnation is also more likely to venture into second mortgages, where another lender already has charge over the assets.

Defence: Be clear on whether you are investing in debentures or unsecured notes, scour the prospectus to ascertain whether you would hold any security over real assets (ie. not just over loans on assets) and find out how deep the issuer's, or its parent's, pockets are. Could it bail you out if the investment went belly up? Finally, only ever invest a small percentage of your assets in these products.

Useful websites

Websites that give information on scams:
www.asic.gov.au
www.fido.asic.gov.au
www.scamwatch.gov.au

Consumer rights:
www.consumer.gov.au

Notes:

Step 9
Protect what you've amassed

Brace yourself – we're about to embark on probably the most unglamorous part of your finances: insurance. But, to my mind, it's one of the most important. After all, there is absolutely no point putting all this effort into building your personal wealth if an untoward event could leave it in tatters.

A word on general insurance

At the most fundamental, make sure you insure any asset you either own or – even more importantly – are in the process of paying off. This means car insurance, contents insurance and insurance for what is probably your single biggest investment, your home.

But it is not enough simply to *have* this insurance – you must have *enough* to replace your possessions or rebuild your house. This was a lesson the unfortunate people whose homes were destroyed in the 2003 bushfires in Canberra learned only too well. A report by the Australian Securities and Investments Commission found they were between 27 per cent and 40 per cent underinsured on average – a shortfall that left many unable to rebuild.

> There is absolutely no point putting all this
> effort into building your personal wealth if an
> untoward event could leave it in tatters

The regulator estimates that, in the wider population, at least 27 per cent and possibly as many as 81 per cent of homeowners are underinsured by 10 per cent or more.

The only way to know for certain that you have the right level of cover is to get a quantity surveyor in to assess the replacement cost of your home and any investment properties. Should anything go wrong, it could be well worth the expense.

Risk insurance

Next, take a close look at what's called risk insurance – insurance that covers you and your family if you have an accident, become ill or, perish the thought, die. The more debts you have, the more important this becomes.

If you have dependants, life insurance is a must. This, of course, pays a lump sum to your beneficiaries if you die. Check your super scheme – it's likely to give you some level of cover. Ideally, however, you want enough to pay out your debts and perhaps cover your dependants' living expenses for a time (if, for example, your partner would have to stay at home to look after the kids, and would therefore receive no income).

Often life insurance is sold with total and permanent disability insurance. This pays a lump sum on – you guessed it – total and permanent disability. It's usually quite cheap and so well worth investigating.

The final type of risk insurance I believe is important (you would be working simply to pay your premiums if you bought *everything* that was on offer) is income protection insurance. This is insurance that will replace up to 75 per cent of your salary if accident or illness leaves you unable to work. It is particularly important if you have dependants and haven't yet paid off your home. As an added bonus, it is also tax deductible.

But be warned, income protection insurance is expensive. You can reduce the cost by selecting a longer waiting period – say three or six months – before payments commence. Make sure it will pay out until age 65, though – there's no use buying a policy that will cease payments after just two years if you are decades away from retirement.

In general, risk insurance is not the place to scrimp as a policy that's never going to pay out is a total waste of your money. And, whatever you do, never sign up for insurance that doesn't have the words 'guaranteed renewable' in the fine print. This means that even if your health deteriorates over the course of a year, you will be able to sign up for the policy the following year.

Wealth watch

Instead of purchasing income protection insurance, many people have earmarked the additional money they've built up in their mortgage to tide them over should they lose their income for any reason. The idea is that if you are ahead and you get into financial strife, you could stop repayments for a while. Or you could redraw what you have overpaid, and drip feed it back in.

This is a perfectly valid strategy – but make sure you actually *can*.

Many loan contracts do not allow repayment holidays, even if you have built up a buffer. And redraw is a facility offered only on some loans. In fact, mortgages can be like one-way traps.

For instance, if you take a repayment holiday when you have additional money sitting on your mortgage, that additional money is likely to be 'swallowed up'. Lenders could well recalculate your repayments at the end of the holiday on a balance that includes your overpayments.

Worse still, if you actually *do* have a loan that allows redraws but you lose your job, many lenders will stop you from taking out overpayments, preferring to keep that money to protect themselves. (Of course, you have to *tell* them before they can freeze your money …)

In a nutshell, stop paying extra into your mortgage if there's even a chance you mightn't be able to get it back. Use an offset account linked to the loan instead (but make sure it's a 100 per cent offset and that the rate is competitive). As mentioned in Step 2, this will also work in your favour if down the track you decide to convert your home into an investment property, as you will be able to withdraw the money *and* retain tax deductions.

Protecting your health

As a health insurance actuary (a scary breed indeed!) once said to me, you'd have to be crazy not to have health insurance.

This is because you can do everything right – eat correctly, exercise regularly and abstain from smoking – and still contract cancer or be hit by a car. Without private health cover, you would have to throw yourself on the mercy of the public system, which (sorry to be morbid) might not get to you soon enough.

And despite what some commentators say, often self-insuring – saving the equivalent of your premiums into an account designated for medical expenses – wouldn't help. The average big medical procedure costs $100,000 and the average huge procedure $250,000. So if you are unlucky enough to need one of these, you won't have the money even if you diligently squirreled away what you would have paid in premiums.

Yes, you could go through your whole life without making a significant claim on your health insurance. But then you might have to claim 100, 1000 or even 100,000 times the premiums you paid. There's just no way of predicting it.

And don't forget, unless you have cover, you will also pay extra tax if you are a single person earning more than $50,000 a year or a couple earning more than $100,000.

Sure, health insurance is expensive – and the gap between what procedures cost and how much the insurance will pay out is getting larger and larger. But the alternative doesn't bear thinking about.

Top tips

> With house insurance, do not calculate your required cover by deducting the value of your land from the purchase price of your property. This is likely to produce a figure insufficient to rebuild. And, if you are tempted to under-insure to save on premiums, consider choosing a higher excess instead. At least then you'll know the extent of what you would be up for.

> Remember to increase your buildings insurance if you renovate – and *immediately*. After all, the rebuild cost will increase with your spend. Also make sure that, at the very least, your sum insured is adjusted each year for inflation. But be aware that the cost of rebuilding often increases more rapidly than this.

> Make sure that your home contents policy includes public liability insurance, and that this applies outside of your house. There have been some awful situations where people have been personally liable for accidents that occur, for example, on the golf course.

> If you are 30 or under, seriously consider taking out health insurance. For every year you wait after 30, your premiums will be 2 per cent higher, up to a maximum of 70 per cent.

> While the cost of health insurance increases every year, you might find you can get a better deal with a different provider. Just check the coverage is identical (or adequate) and make sure there is no waiting period. You could also cut your premiums by choosing a higher excess. While you will be up for money each time you have to have a procedure, at least you will be covered for any big medical problems.

> If you are considering starting a family, make sure you apply for obstetrics cover at least one year before you intend the baby being born. Wait until after conception and you won't be covered. By the same token, check how long before the birth you need to switch to a family policy for your child to be covered.

> Don't go anywhere without travel insurance – you are just tempting fate. But make sure the policy you buy is a good one. Check particularly that it offers decent cover in all of your destinations and know the exclusions. Finally, avoid buying your insurance through a travel agent because they receive large commissions – sometimes more than 50 per cent – out of your premiums. As a result, you could pay far too much. Surf the net to buy direct from insurers or from resellers.

Dirty tricks

> Unless an insurance company-operated calculator designed to determine the rebuild cost of your home asks 20 to 30 questions, the chances are it will underestimate the rebuild cost. In fact, in a test of online calculators by ASIC, the highest estimate was more than two and a half times the lowest estimate – for the same house in the same location!

Defence: Find a company with a rigorous approach or hire a quantity surveyor to give you an accurate quote.

> Income protection is an absolute minefield and I have heard so many heartbreaking stories of insurers refusing to pay out.

Defence: Go through the small print with a fine-tooth comb and know exactly what you are and what you are not covered for. Also beware of any obligations you have under the policy, such as to disclose all medical information up to the point your insurance is approved, which can take several months. Finally, keep evidence of your salary at the time you apply for the insurance – if you ever need to make a claim, it is at *this* point that you will have to prove it.

> Watch out for the interaction of income protection insurance with total and permanent disability insurance. One often cancels the other out! Some insurers treat any lump sum payment from TPD as income received over a particular number, say eight, years. They then offset this against your income protection payments, so that you might receive nothing for the first eight years.

Defence: Take out only quality policies that do not offset TPD payments.

> I could devote reams to insurance in super – but don't worry, I won't. There are just a few main traps you need to know about.

1. If you leave any life insurance you have in super to anyone other than your financial dependants, they will be taxed heavily.

Defence: Buy separate life cover for these beneficiaries.

2. If the amount of money you have in super and the amount of any insurance you hold within the fund exceeds $1.3 million, your heirs will be taxed on the excess.

Defence: If you are lucky enough to be in this ball park, take out life insurance outside of super.

3. Beware of TPD in super. Your super fund might have much stricter payout rules than your actual insurer – so you might get a payout only to find it is locked away until you are 55 or 60. This situation is so common that it accounts for about 30 per cent of complaints to the Superannuation Complaints Tribunal – but the vast majority of decisions go in favour of the super fund and against the insured person.

Defence: Do not take out TPD within super. It's not worth the risk.

4. Under super rules, income protection policies pay out for a maximum of two years.

Defence: Buy a policy outside of super with a two-year waiting period, or don't hold income protection within super at all.

Useful websites

Insurance comparisons:
   www.insurancewatch.com.au

Health insurance brokers:
   www.health-link.com.au and www.iselect.com.au

Insurance information:
   www.apra.gov.au (Australian Prudential Regulation Authority).

Step 10
Take a gamble

As I said earlier in the piece, the road to wealth is a slow and steady one – that is, unless you win lotto or some other big-prize competition. So why not take a ticket every once in a while and surrender yourself to the fantasy of winning, rather than earning, your fortune?

Just before you rush out and blow your carefully constructed budget, though, I should qualify the above statement. Taking this ticket needs to leave you in a *financially neutral* position. In other words, you need to give up something of the equivalent value. For example, if you want to spend $5 on a raffle ticket, you could bring your lunch from home instead of buying it. If you want to spend $3 on lotto, cut out a coffee.

They say to never gamble more than you can afford to lose – but if all you are gambling is money you would otherwise have eaten or drunk, there's no skin off your nose if your numbers *never* come up. Simply treat it as a bit of fun. Be pleasantly surprised if you win, but expect to lose – because the chances are that you will …

Wealth box

On Saturday night the odds of winning a division one prize from a 12-game Lotto entry (the most popular entry) are 1 in 678,755. In OZ Lotto, the odds of winning from an eight-game entry (again, the most popular entry) are 1 in 1,018,133.

The best way to give yourself a higher chance of winning is to take systems entries, where you can choose more than the standard amount of numbers. In both Saturday lotto and OZ Lotto, a System 8 will improve your odds to 1 in 290,895, while a System 9 will improve them to 1 in 96,965 (source: Tattersall's Lotteries).

Top tips

> With lotto, don't avoid choosing numbers in the 40s just because there are less of these. They are just as likely to come up.

> Similarly, don't choose more odd than even numbers on the basis that there are 23 odds and 22 evens. Every number has an equal chance of being drawn.

> Many people choose their lotto numbers based on birthdays, so you may find you have to share any prize with fewer people if you go instead for numbers above 31.

Useful websites:

For help with a gambling problem:
www.reachout.com.au.

Good luck – but just in case the big prize never comes your way, don't forget to save, save, SAVE!

The Final Word

So there you have it — the 10 Steps that will give you the very best chance of doubling your wealth and halving your worries.

To recap:

Step 1: Get your relationship with money right

Step 2: Know your debt intimately

Step 3: Make every cent you can

Step 4: Keep every cent you can

Step 5: Reward yourself

Step 6: Invest smart

Step 7: Use the system to help rather than hinder you

Step 8: Don't let anyone sabotage you

Step 9: Protect what you've amassed

Step 10: Take a gamble

But if I had to sum it all up in just one word, that word would be *focus*. Know what you want and do all you can to achieve it. There is no better way to ensure your success.

Just don't forget to keep it all in perspective. There are far more important things than money. In fact, wealth building should not be your ultimate goal at all – your ultimate goal should be attaining the freedom that comes with it.

Take care,

Nicole

Notes: